NEW GENESIS

In praise of NEW GENESIS . . .

"[Robert Muller's] message is not intended for the Christian faith alone but embraces all religions. This book will give its readers courage for life and hope for the future of our world."

—*American Library Association*

"Lots of food for thought and spiritual nourishment here. If you want to probe a spirituality grounded in compassion, reality, and hope, read and reread NEW GENESIS."

—*Sisters Today*

"It is rewarding indeed to find a book, a voice, that cries out not with distress but with hope. Let us hope that Mr. Muller's vision is contagious and we may catch his optimistic perspective that the world is working at solving its problems, that progress is being made on all fronts."

—*The A.R.E. Journal*

"We find in NEW GENESIS chapters on the need for World Gratitude, the Issue of Human Rights, the Need for Global Education, and so much more that we warmly recommend you to read the rich thought forms of this extraordinary, indeed unique man—Robert Muller—yourself."

—*The New Humanity*

"This is a heartening and broadening book that opens into a larger, more comprehensive biosphere. It deserves special attention."

—*Adris Newletter*

"The book retains its cohesiveness, provides a glimpse of a fascinating and inspiring individual, and encourages the reader to adopt—and act upon— an expanded world view. Good reading for adults concerned with the world-wide situation!"

—*Christian Bookseller & Librarian*

Also by Robert Muller

MOST OF ALL THEY TAUGHT ME HAPPINESS

NEW GENESIS
Shaping a Global Spirituality

Robert Muller

COMPLETE AND UNABRIDGED

IMAGE BOOKS
A DIVISION OF
DOUBLEDAY & COMPANY, INC.
GARDEN CITY, NEW YORK

Image Books edition published March 1984 by special arrangement with Doubleday & Company, Inc.

"The UN's Prophet of Hope" by Pam Robbins originally appeared in the September 1979 issue of *Sign* Magazine, copyright © 1979 by Passionist Missions, Inc. Used by permission of the publisher.

"My Five Teilhardian Enlightenments" originally appeared in *The Spirit of the Earth,* by Jerome Pulinski (Seabury Press, 1980). Reprinted by permission of the publisher.

Library of Congress Cataloging in Publication Data

Muller, Robert.
New Genesis.

1. Spirituality. I. Title.
BV4501.2.M76   261.8
        AACR2
ISBN: 0-385-19332-7
Library of Congress Catalog Card Number 81-43925

I dedicate this book to the innumerable good people of this planet who want to live in peace, friendship, freedom and justice, and to enjoy the miracle of life under the generous rays of our sun and the good guidance of the God of the universe.

It is dedicated to all peacemakers who try to heal the antiquated quarrels, divisions and insanity of those who refuse to recognize the oneness of our planetary home and of the human family.

It is dedicated to all my comrades from Alsace-Lorraine who died in the flower of their age during World War II while God granted me the privilege of survival.

It is dedicated to the United Nations, the first universal organization of this planet, from which I have learned so much.

It is dedicated to Dag Hammarskjöld and U Thant, my spiritual masters.

It is dedicated to all those who have given me peace, happiness, love and knowledge during my sojourn on earth.

May the kind divine providence help us start a new history and prepare the advent of a new age, a new world, a new philosophy and new human relationships, as we approach the bimillennium.

Let us all coalesce with all our strength, mind, heart and soul around a New Genesis, a true global, God-abiding political, moral and spiritual renaissance to make this planet at long last what it was always meant to be: the Planet of God.

Robert Muller

Contents

PART IV: MY PERSONAL GLOBAL
TRANSCENDENCE

FOREWORD

The UN's Prophet of Hope
by Pam Robbins

Pam Robbins is a free-lance journalist writing on religious and humanistic subjects. She lives in Springfield, Massachusetts.

NEW YORK CITY—His office on the twenty-ninth floor of the United Nations Secretariat building gives him a view of more than the skyline. For over thirty years he has witnessed conflicts, crises, natural and man-made disasters around the world.

But Robert Muller remains undaunted. His round face is smiling and his blue eyes serene as he declares cheerfully, "A new world is in the making."

This is not the assessment of one whose ignorance is bliss. Currently serving as Secretary of the UN's Economic and Social Council, Muller has filled numerous posts for the organization, including that of aide to three Secretaries-General. He holds degrees in law and economics from the universities of Strasbourg and Heidelberg and from Columbia University. A native of Belgium who was raised in Alsace-Lorraine, he fought in the French Resistance and was briefly imprisoned by the Nazis.

Muller has collected some of his adventures and insights in a book titled, *Most of All They Taught Me Happiness*.[1] "People who live in the world of action," he explains, too often postpone writing until some future date which never arrives. "Rather than leave nothing behind," he decided to record "a few perspectives, recipes for happi-

[1] New York: Doubleday & Co., Inc., 1978.

ness. I have tested them and maybe one will be appropriate for you."

Despite the well-cut gray suit, striped tie, crisp white handkerchief peeking from his breast pocket, and a golden Crucifix given to him by Pope John Paul II, there is a simplicity about the man. He could as easily be the hatmaker his father was. The austere office he occupies is enlivened by pieces of sculpture on walls and surfaces, and by his own energy and enthusiasm.

Like his book, his conversation is pervaded by unbounded optimism. "I saw a film on television last night, *The Grapes of Wrath*. It is a description of what happened during the thirties in the dust bowl. When you see it, you immediately realize what a distance has been covered. That could not happen today." It is the observation of a man who persists in believing the glass is half full, while all around him call it half empty. "Never in human life is the situation completely satisfactory, but you must have the ability of looking back and forward. People are often dissatisfied because they do not take stock of what they have accomplished.

"In 1948, when I first came here, there was not a single black nurse in any hospital in New York, not a single black teller in any bank. I was appalled. We have made tremendous gains in racial equality." Reading the will and testament of George Washington recently, he discovered that the first President had bequeathed a number of slaves to his wife. "And that was George Washington! We are still far from a perfect world, but we must keep at it. Progress, even if it is not satisfactory, is nonetheless progress. Every hour six thousand people die, but that doesn't prevent doctors from trying to save lives."

For Muller, optimism is more than an inherent disposition; it is an obligation, a responsibility. "In order to model a happy and beautiful world," he has written, "we must believe in it, we must work at it; we must be in love with it." Teachers and others will say "some children are optimistically or pessimistically inclined. As with all life, you are born with certain natural tendencies, but you can change them. If you could not, you could just forget about education.

"When you sit in my position, you know what is going on in the world and the time is getting ripe to restore confidence." His book, he points out, is only one of several on similar topics of hope and positivism and his friend Norman Cousins (of *Saturday Review* fame) "is going all over the United States making speeches in which he says the world is divided not into East and West, or rich and poor, or black and white, but into optimists and pessimists." He chuckles as he recalls his attendance earlier this year at a conference of missionaries from various religions. "When I finished my speech, one missionary said, 'How can you be so optimistic? What are your reasons!' I looked at him. 'I am not an expert on optimism,' I told him. 'You are. It is called the miracle of faith. All the religions are based on that.'"

The linking of optimism and faith may explain Muller's fascination with religion and his conviction that it is through the world's religions and their belief that life is sacred that global problems can be solved.

"My great personal dream is to get a tremendous alliance between all the major religions and the UN. U Thant used to say we would not be able to solve our problems without seeing our place in relation to the universe."

Muller is a Catholic and considers himself a good one. "But I am not so fanatical as not to respect other faiths. I would never fight with another religion about the superiority of mine." He recalls one of his four children asking him, "What is the best religion?" His reply is the one he gives anyone who asks a similar question. "You have about five thousand religions on the planet," he says. "You'd be dead before you studied them all to decide which is the best. You are born into a religion and it will give you full satisfaction. Be interested in all religions, in what they have in common, but there is no compelling reason to switch.

"I have a little file of things on particular religions that would be good for everyone." He picks up a folder and begins thumbing through until he locates a paper on Moslem dietary rules. "They explain the prohibition of alcohol because intoxication hinders people from remembrance of God and the proper observance of their prayers." His excitement is obvious. Deeply troubled by the worldwide tide of alcohol abuse, Muller believes the only answer lies in "linking it to God, saying, 'If you want to be in communion with God, you cannot be intoxicated. Period.'" Moslems pray at least five times a day, he continues. "You know how they explain it? They say that you drink water several times a day; you have the same need to drink the water of God. Common sense." He remembers a world conference on water during which he longed to hang a sentence from the Koran above the assembly hall: "Do not waste a drop of water, even if you are sitting on the bank of a river." A simple statement, he says, "but it says it all. Scientists and people in government would be well advised to turn to religions to ask their perceptions and guidance. And religions should urgently assimilate the tremendous results of science and accelerate their ecumenic, global cooperation. They are far behind nations in that respect."

People often evaluate the United Nations and the Catholic Church in the same light, he says, since both are world-wide in scope, prize human life, and seek what is ultimately good for humanity. Critics often dismiss both as lofty, unrealistic and ineffective in achieving their goals of peace and brotherhood. Muller disagrees. "In my opinion, they are both extremely effective—in the long run. They are part of building the ethics and evolution of humanity." Neither body can offer instant remedies, but that does not mean they achieve nothing. He uses a UN example. "Say you begin to notice that the actions of all the nations are damaging the seas and oceans. You call a world conference and governments immediately begin to wake up. There are now ministries of the environment everywhere. You don't see things improve overnight, but the rate of deterioration begins to diminish." Full improvement only comes with time, but historians, he maintains, "will say that at the turning point of the nineteen hundred seventies, when so many global problems arose, humanity was lucky to have global organizations.

"I would hate to think what the world would be today if, during the last thirty years of population explosion, atomic bombs, increased science and technology, nations hadn't had a place to meet. We would have had at least two world wars in that period." He admits that the UN has often failed. In preventing conflicts, for instance, he rates its success as fifty-fifty, not very good for a peace-keeping organization. But, in the tremendously dangerous period when Asian and African states sought independence, the UN reduced bloodshed by ninety per cent, and the picture of racism would be far uglier if there were none of the black delegates speaking out in the UN forum.

The organization has provided an enormous service in preventing the coalition of poor countries by giving them a place to let off steam and to obtain help. This outlet has prevented a splitting of the world into rich and poor, which would mean world disaster. Both the political center in New York and the thirty-two agencies of the UN are writing the future. "What you are reading on the front page of the newspapers is being forged here," Muller says.

His positive evaluation of the UN's past is matched by an equally upbeat forecast for the organization and the world it serves. "There will be no third world war between the big powers," he says matter-of-factly. "They are so interlinked and armed that a war is unthinkable. But there will be conflicts between poor countries. One of my major recommendations is to foster cooperation between the developing countries, to turn their energies away from territory and power to more constructive objectives."

He does not, however, see quick disarmament. Nations are "too insecure for that. Several decades will pass before that progress can be made." Again, he expects a gradual shift, beginning with a slow de-escalation of arms build-up. Also on a negative side, he predicts "continued human rights violations in many countries. Another major problem—until the year 2000—will be the poor. Population will increase from four and a half billion to six billion and ninety per cent will be born in developing countries. Not even an economic miracle will solve that." Generally, the world will have to deal with global problems—population, environment, natural resources. "We have to manage our planet with more intelligence. By the year 2000 we will be fully into the business of making a new world." The task of doing so does not require any form of world government, he stresses, although narrow nationalism will shrink and countries will become "like Vermont and California are now. Things do not come into being in terms of world law, but at the end of a meeting on terrorism or the law of the sea, for example, delegates go home and write national legislation. They prefer to do it that way, and it doesn't matter. We can do the job with that. It is the result that counts."

Muller often refers to an exchange of letters between Albert Einstein and Sigmund Freud, in which a frustrated Einstein asked the psychologist if he could offer any answers to the problems of armament, aggression and war. Freud's reply noted that humans are divided between instincts of aggression and love. Peace would require the development of ties of sentiment among people. "The love of country has succeeded in binding people at the national level. The great new historical challenge is to develop love among all earth inhabitants, and for the earth itself."

Muller firmly believes such unity among humankind can be

achieved. "This was the message of God—you can do it, but it's up
to you to do it," he says. One of the most significant aspects of
Christ's message to the world, he believes, is that Christ "always, un-
compromisingly was on the side of light, not darkness, good, not
evil. There was no yin and yang in Christ." He also remained true to
his message "right to the end. He let himself be killed," Muller says,
stabbing the air with a forefinger for emphasis, "rather than fight his
killers with their own methods."

It is a lesson which Muller has taken to heart. His world view has
earned him various epithets, even from his admirers. But those who
say he is somehow "different" are only "seeking an excuse" for not
embracing his positive attitude. As he told one woman, "There are
40,000 international civil servants. Even if you came to me and said
39,999 are no-good bureaucrats, I am not going to change one little
bit. Why should you let yourself be reduced by the behavior of
others? You have one power, the power over yourself. As an individual, you might be pushed down or pushed forward."

Dealing in global proportions has made him even more convinced
of the power and responsibility of each person. "The most important act of the individual is to take good care of his own life. We
have a planet of four and a half billion people. It will be a good
planet if there are four and a half billion good, peaceful and happy
people. The total situation depends, in the end, not on governments
and on the UN but on the people. You cannot expect the world to
change before you change yourself."

Such self-determination must be rooted in a spiritual value system
and Muller has found ample inspiration in the lives of people he has
known, including Dag Hammarskjöld and U Thant. Hammarskjöld
was a dedicated servant of Sweden before coming to the UN. But it
was there that he became "one of the great mystics of our time. I
read every day the same book he read, *The Imitation of Christ*, a
recipe for spiritual life for a man of action, an ideal book for an international civil servant. Hammarskjöld showed the world that the
way to sanctity passes through the world of action."

U Thant, a Buddhist whom Muller calls "a master in the art of
living," never drew distinctions between his public and spiritual
lives, but instead lived the former in accordance with the precepts of
the latter. Muller attempts to do the same. "A man must care to
know during his lifetime how he wants to be remembered in death.
This will mold his entire life," he has written, and he wants to be

remembered as "having tried to convince everybody I could that to be alive on this planet is a miracle."

Muller is fully aware of the uniqueness of his life and the people he has known during it. That awareness compels him to write and speak. "I will retire in a few years, and if God allows, I see my life very clearly. Now that I am getting older, I have to leave to others the lessons left to me. I have had a complete adult life in the first universal organization, working only for the world and humanity, according to the oath I took when I entered the United Nations. I am not the same being as in 1948, when I first came here. I have been given so much and it is absolutely my duty to give it back in digested form—speeches, articles, books. My great duty is to conclude." He glances out the wide window at the New York panorama. "There is," he says simply, "a lot of happiness in store for me."

NEW GENESIS

PART I

The Global Transcendence
of Humanity

PART I

The Cosmic Consequences
of Heresy

1

The Need for Global Education

In order to prepare our children properly for tomorrow's world, we must discern among the agitations and headlines of the day those trends and tendencies which are fundamental to our time and put aside whatever is accidental, secondary, ephemeral and anachronistic.

What strikes us most in recent years is that, since the last world war, humankind has entered a totally new era of history, perhaps even of evolution. During this period man has advanced dramatically into the infinitely large and the infinitely small. More scientific progress has been achieved in the last thirty years than during the entire previous history of mankind. Instruments, linked by instant communication to our planet, have been sent farther and farther away into the universe. Humans have set foot on the moon and have returned safely to earth. Outer space is being used for unprecedented systems of world-wide communication and study of the earth's resources and physical conditions. More than two thousand satellites and space objects are circling around the earth. Transportation has expanded from land and sea to the atmosphere, with ever larger and faster planes. Man has reached with his tools the abyss of the seas. We have witnessed the harnessing of atomic energy, the birth of electronics, of cybernetics, of laser technology and the unlocking of many mysteries of the infinitely small. Microbiology has opened up new exhilarating and frightening vistas of scientific advance with the synthesis of genes. Never on this planet has there been such intensive research and discovery by so many scientists in so many lands.

The Industrial Revolution and its recent scientific and techno-

logical acceleration have had far-reaching consequences for humankind. The first effect was an unprecedented improvement in living
conditions on our planet. This improvement is spreading progressively to the entire world despite regrettable discrepancies and de-
lays.

Length of life has increased, reaching more than seventy years in
many affluent societies. Even in India life expectancy has increased
from forty to fifty years in two decades. Diseases which caused great
epidemics not long ago have been wiped out. Gigantic efforts are
being made to attack the remaining principal causes of early death.
Thus humanity's death rate has been reduced from 17 per 1,000 in
1950-55 to 13 per 1,000 in 1965-77. The world is able to feed more
than one million additional people a week. During the last twenty
years more than six hundred million newcomers have been added to
the world's literate population.

The goods placed at the command of people for their sustenance
and enjoyment have reached phenomenal quantities in some societies. Thus, to sustain a person in the United States over an average
life span, 56 million gallons of water, 37,000 gallons of gasoline, 5½
tons of meat, 5½ tons of wheat, 9 tons of milk and cream are
required. In the poorer parts of the world the level of consumption
is only a fraction of such figures. But there, too, the amount of
goods placed at the disposal of the individual is on the increase. The
scientific and technical revolution which started two hundred years
ago has spread to most continents and it will encompass, in the not
too distant future, our entire planet.

Its second effect has been the advent of an entirely new period in
world history, namely, the era of mass phenomena due to the multi-
plication of human lives. Lower death rates, longer lives and better
lives have brought about the well-known accelerated growth of the
human race.

People on our planet have increased from 2.5 billion in 1951,
when the UN published the first world statistics, to 4.5 billion in
1980. We will be more than 6 billion people in the year 2000 and a
child being born today might live in a world of 8 billion at the age
of sixty. It is as if the child were to witness the landing of several billion more people on this planet during his lifetime.

The statistics published by the United Nations and its specialized
agencies show a doubling or tripling of most world data during the
past twenty years. World industrial production has tripled. The vol-

ume of world exports has quadrupled. Agricultural production has increased 1.7 times. The phenomenal growth in the production of certain commodities is illustrated by petroleum, which has increased 5 times, plastic, which has increased 15 times, aluminum 5 times, cement 4 times, crude steel 2.8 times, motor vehicles 2.7 times. There were only 11 cities of more than one million inhabitants in 1923; there are 160 today and there will be more than 300 in the year 2000, 40 of which will have more than 10 million inhabitants.

While the population increase is greatest in the poorer countries and the consumption explosion greatest in the developed ones, the Industrial Revolution will continue its world-wide spread. Higher population figures will then be accompanied by higher consumption everywhere, yielding staggering results. This is the new world into which we have entered. These are the real causes of the various crises which have lately beset our planet: pressures on the environment, on resources, the energy crisis, the food crisis, the urban crisis, and inflation.

The third effect has been the advent of an intricate and extremely dense network of world-wide interdependencies among societies which until recently were living in relative isolation from each other. Beyond nature's interdependencies which have always characterized our planet (the water cycle, the oxygen cycle, the carbon cycle, the nitrogen cycle, and many other internal links of the biosphere), the world has suddenly been seized in a rapidly growing web of man-made interdependencies. Thousands of planes are constantly in the air, and at certain airports they sometimes wait in queues for the opening of an air channel. Thousands of ships and trains are carrying huge quantities of goods from one country to another. Some seaports cannot catch up with the increase in world trade. International tourism, congresses, meetings, assistance and studies are mushrooming. Colossal transnational companies have a foot in many countries, combining money, labor, resources and technologies across national boundaries on a world-wide scale, and taking the globe as a single market. They begin to dwarf many nations, thus opening yet another page in the history of power.

These interdependencies have forced governments into new collective thinking and cooperative arrangements which would have been inconceivable only a few decades ago. The United Nations, as a result, has profoundly changed. The world organization, strengthened by thirty-two specialized agencies and world programs, is today concerned with practically every global problem on earth.

Through its world-wide data collection, studies and conferences—political, economic, social, scientific, cultural and environmental—the United Nations has become the greatest observatory and warning system of planet Earth. Through it, governments are making an honest effort at cooperation in many fields, although such cooperation would warrant infinitely more heart, effort, vision and generosity.

Under such dramatically changed circumstances, which deeply affect our lives, there is an urgent need for more *global education*. This is very important for the future of humanity. How can our children go to school and learn so much detail about the past, the geography and the administration of their countries and so little about the world, its global problems, its interdependencies, its future and its international institutions? People are astonished by the sudden emergence of global crises. They wonder how environmental deterioration could have developed to the point of endangering life on this planet. They wonder why there is an energy crisis which had not been foreseen by their governments (but had been foreseen by the United Nations, which convened, as early as 1961, the first world conference on new sources of energy). They ask themselves why bad crops in faraway countries should make the prices of the food on their tables shoot up and why there is a sudden world food shortage after so many years of agricultural surpluses (again nations had been warned of the danger by the UN's Food and Agriculture Organization). A child born today will be faced as an adult, almost daily, with problems of a global interdependent nature, be it peace, food, the quality of life, inflation, or scarcity of resources. He will be both an actor and a beneficiary or a victim in the total world fabric, and he may rightly ask: "Why was I not warned? Why was I not better educated? Why did my teachers not tell me about these problems and indicate my behavior as a member of an interdependent human race?" It is, therefore, the duty and the self-enlightened interest of governments to educate their children properly about the type of world in which they are going to live. They must inform the children of the actions, the endeavors and the recommendations of their global organizations. They must be prepared to assume responsibility for the consequences of their actions and help in the care of several billion more fellow humans on earth. Many governments have begun to realize this. In 1974 they created a United Nations University located in Tokyo, with affiliates in many countries. In 1979 the UN General Assembly welcomed the decision by the government of Costa Rica to establish a University of Peace. Institutes for global education have sprung up, and the UN and UNESCO are convening meetings of educators to develop global curricula. In many countries, especially the United States, educators feel that this is a new educational trend whose time has come.

The United Nations and its specialized agencies have a wealth of data and knowledge on every conceivable world problem. This source must be systematically tapped by educators. Time is running short. Global events are moving fast. It would be more beneficial to teach children around the world to close their water faucets a few seconds earlier, and to conserve our resources, than to adopt intricate legislation or endlessly drill new holes in the ground. The world will be in great trouble and will not be able to solve its global problems if citizens are not taught properly from their earliest youth. This is a great new challenge, a new historical dimension, and a thrilling objective for educators everywhere in the world.

Beyond the turmoil, the divisions and perplexities of our time, humanity is slowly but surely finding the ways, limits and new codes of behavior which will encompass all races, nations, religions and ideologies. It is the formulation of these new ethics which will be the great challenge for the new generation. It will concern not only man's material fate but also his mental and spiritual lives. The fulfillment of a human person's earthly destiny, of his happiness during his short span of life, of his right place in creation, depends in great degree on his comprehension of the total web of life and his personal part and comportment in it. Former Secretary-General U Thant, a teacher, when discussing these problems, always came back to his fundamental belief that education held the keys to the future, and that mental fulfillment was superior to material life, moral qualities superior to mental qualities, and spiritual fulfillment superior to mental life. In a speech he made on his religious beliefs in Toronto in 1966, he said:

"The law of love and compassion for all living creatures is again a doctrine to which we are all too ready to pay lip-service. However, if it is to become a reality, it requires a process of education, a veritable mental renaissance. Once it has become a reality, national as well as international problems will fall into perspective and become easier to solve. Wars and conflicts, too, will then become a thing of the past, because wars begin in the minds of men, and in those minds love and compassion would have built the defences of peace."

In his farewell address to the United Nations in December 1971, he said:

". . . I have certain priorities in regard to virtues and human values. An ideal man, or an ideal woman, is one who is endowed with four attributes, four qualities—physical, intellectual, moral and spiritual qualities. Of course it is very rare to find a human being who is endowed with all these qualities but, as far as priorities are concerned, I would attach greater importance to intellectual qualities over physical qualities. I would attach still greater importance to moral qualities over intellectual qualities. It is far from my intention to denigrate intellectualism, but I would attach greater importance to moral qualities or moral virtues over intellectual virtues—moral qualities like love, compassion, understanding, tolerance, the philosophy of 'live and let live,' the ability to understand the other person's point of view, which are the key to all great religions. And above all I would attach the greatest importance to spiritual values, spiritual qualities. I deliberately avoid using the term 'religion.' I have in mind the spiritual virtues, faith in oneself, the purity of one's inner self which to me is the greatest virtue of all. With this approach, with this philosophy, with this concept alone, will we be able to fashion the kind of society we want, the society which was envisaged by the founding fathers of the United Nations."

Yes, global education must transcend material, scientific and intellectual achievements and reach deliberately into the moral and spiritual spheres. Man has been able to extend the power of his hands with incredible machines, of his eyes with telescopes and microscopes, of his ears with telephones, radio and sonars, of his brain with computers and automation. He must now also extend his heart, his sentiments, his love and his soul to the entire human family, to the planet, to the stars, to the universe, to eternity and to God.

He must perceive his right, miraculous place in the splendor of God's creation. We must manage our globe so as to permit the endless stream of humans admitted to the miracle of life to fulfill their lives physically, mentally, morally and spiritually as has never been possible before in our entire evolution. Global education must prepare our children for the coming of an interdependent, safe, prosperous, friendly, loving, happy planetary age as has been heralded by all great prophets. The real, the great period of human fulfillment on planet Earth is only now about to begin.

A PARABLE[1]

Once upon a time there was a class
and the students expressed disapproval of their teacher.
Why should they be concerned with
global interdependency, global problems
and what others of the world were thinking, feeling and doing?
And the teacher said she had a dream in which she
saw one of her students fifty years from today.
The student was angry and said,
"Why did I learn so much detail about the past
and the administration of my country
and so little about the world?"
He was angry because no one told him
that as an adult he would be faced
almost daily with problems of a
global interdependent nature, be they
problems of peace, security, quality
of life, food, inflation, or scarcity
of natural resources.
The angry student found he was the
victim as well as the beneficiary.
"Why was I not warned? Why was
I not better educated? Why
did my teachers not tell me about
the problems and help me understand
I was a member of an interdependent human race?"
With even greater anger the student shouted,
"You helped me extend my hands with incredible machines,
my eyes with telescopes and microscopes,
my ears with telephones, radios, and sonar,
my brain with computers,
but you did not help me extend
my heart, love, concern
to the entire human family.
You, teacher, gave me half a loaf."

[1] By Jon Rye Kinghorn, based on the preceding essay, from *A Step-by-Step Guide for Conducting a Consensus and Diversity Workshop in Global Education.* A Program of the Commission on Schools, North Central Association and the Charles F. Kettering Foundation.

2

Of Right Human Relations

Someday our planet will be a world spiritual democracy. Today's international community is only an assemblage of powers. How the governors came to power is seldom questioned. At this stage of history, all one can hope for is peace, restraint and cooperation among the tenants of power. But at some point in our evolution the question of the proper representation of the people in the management of our globe will certainly pose itself, as will the spiritual quest for our proper place in the universe and in the eternal stream of time. There is urgent need to determine the cosmic or divine laws which must rule our behavior on earth.

A Sun Safe and Stable

I have now worked in the world organization for over thirty years. I have learned from it more than I would have learned from any university or school on earth, and I continue to learn every day, for the UN has become the greatest laboratory of human affairs that ever was. It is an entirely new event, a paradigm in evolution. I am in charge of the coordination of the specialized agencies. There are today thirty-two specialized agencies and world programs. This is a fact of momentous historical importance. These agencies cover a large array of human concerns, from aviation to the atom, from children to workers, from agriculture to industry, from navigation to trade, from economic development to the environment, from health and science to art and culture. As a result, governments possess today the embryo of a world system of diagnosis, consultation, monitoring, prognosis and action which allows them to deal with old as well as newly emerging planetary problems. These instruments and agencies provide humankind with the most up-to-date, enlightened perceptions. Thus, recently, when reading a document on extra-terrestrial messages published by the UN Outer Space Committee, I learned something quite fundamental. In it, astrophysicists calculated the likelihood of other civilizations in the universe. They started from the billions of galaxies and the more than two hundred billion stars or suns in our own galaxy. They calculated the probability of planets in belts located at a certain distance from stable suns, i.e., stars whose light hydrogen explosions have reached stability.

This is the case of our sun, which will remain safe and stable for another six to eight billion years. In addition to stable solar radiation, life requires a certain size of planet to retain a favorable atmosphere, a certain chemical composition of the surface of the planet and a rather narrow range of temperature, i.e., the planet must be located neither too near nor too far from a sun. After reviewing these factors, the astrophysicists introduce another: the number of civilizations in the universe further depends on the length of life of such civilizations. The longer civilizations are able to survive and to develop, the larger their total number will be in the universe. And then comes this fundamental statement: *the length of life of a civilization depends on its capability to solve environmental and social problems*; the civilization must not destroy itself, soon after it masters the technical means to do so. Our own civilization stands now at this precise crucial threshold. Two momentous questions have indeed been put to us during the last decades:

- How are we going to deal with our environment, how will we manage it and survive and develop in it without destroying certain vital conditions inherited from billions of years of prior evolution?
- How will we manage to live peacefully and cooperatively together among races, nations, cultures and so many other human groups and interests? In particular, will we be able to refrain from using the life-annihilating arms developed to protect, assert, and foster those specific groups produced by history and called nations?

For the astrophysicists, the problem is very simple: either you do it or you don't. If you don't, you will disappear and the universe will not change a bit.

I will deal here with this second problem, namely, that of "right human relations."

At the United Nations I am faced with so many problems, the complexity of which increases every day, that I had to choose between giving up or developing a canvas which permitted me to see a specific problem at its right place within a logical scheme, so that the totality makes sense, as do our individual beings, our planet and our universe despite their respective complexities. To coordinate requires to discern a sense of direction in the complexity. This is quite fundamental. It is like the coordination of our body's movements: out of the complexity of the surrounding environment and the multiple possibilities of the body we must make sense and decide on the right movement. The human body—from eyes to nerves via the brain—has reached such an advanced stage of coordination that these movements are often "automatic," "unconscious" or "instinctive." Someday humanity will reach the same degree of almost instantaneous adaptations, but we are only at the very beginning of that new evolution and learning process. The United Nations has an important part in it.

The framework which I have adopted to classify and store each problem which reaches my desk consists of the following three categories:

- the physical, non-human cosmos;
- the human, social cosmos;
- the personal, individual cosmos.

The physical, non-human cosmos

I include in that cosmos not only the entire physical world but also all other life forms except humans. In other words, we are human beings, members of a well-defined species with its definite characteristics which lives in the particular circumstances and environment of a given planet. Our first knowledge, our first great adventure in evolution, has to do with this outside world, the surroundings, the totality of our planetary conditions and our relations with the sun. We must know our house, our dwelling, our place of abode in the universe and what it has to offer, favorable or detrimental to human life. On that score, the human race has made prodigious progress over its history and more particularly during the last thirty years. Humanity has extended its knowledge of the far reaches of the universe hundreds of times during the last decades and it has penetrated ever deeper into the infinitely small, the atom, the cell, the genes. At each level, at each layer of this prodigious spatial distribution of the physical universe, scientists, technologists, thinkers and researchers are working relentlessly to extend our knowledge and further uncover "reality."

The totality of our current knowledge culminates in the United Nations and in its specialized agencies where governments thus obtain a planetary view of the human environment. As a result, we are beginning to have a pretty comprehensive grasp of our relationships and place on our planet, of the planet itself, and of its place, structure, and functioning in relation to the sun and to the universe.

I am sometimes tempted to draw an enormous table on one of the walls of my office, presenting in a vertical form the layers of our prodigious knowledge from the infinitely large to the infinitely small and showing for each layer how humans are cooperating in their world organizations, where they draw a synthesis and conclusions from all we know. The table would reach from astrophysics and interplanetary science to solar science and outer space, the earth's atmosphere and its layers, the biosphere, the seas and oceans, the continents, the earth's surface and soils, the climate, the world's waters, energy, the earth's crust (minerals, underground water, heat, oil, etc.), the bottoms of the seas, other living species, the microbial, genetic and planktonic world, the infinitely small realm of the atom, its particles and subparticles, etc. Practically nothing has been left out by humans in their search for total comprehension and possible mastery of the surrounding world. A complete Copernican tapestry is thus emerging for which humanity deserves a high mark among the civilizations in the universe. We have taken stock on an all-planetary scale of this total knowledge in a series of remarkable world conferences held during recent years: on outer space, science and technology, the world's seas and oceans, the environment, water, food and deserts, to mention only those which were concerned with our physical environment. They were the first world conferences ever held on this planet. The fact that all nations on earth were able to cooperate in these tremendous ventures augurs well for our future civilization. They mark the beginning of a science of planetary management which has become all the more necessary now that our actions are able to change the earth so profoundly.

The Human or Social Cosmos

We have also accomplished progress with regard to the human or social cosmos. All the people on earth constitute together an entity, a family, a society. Regarding the quantitative aspects of that society, we have made considerable progress: we had a world population conference; we know how many we are; we know where we live; we know how long we live; and we have projections of the future for the next hundred years. The UN's work on demography is another signal achievement of the new global institutions.

The UN has surveyed every possible quantifiable aspect of humanity: sexes, races, children, youth, old age, the number of malnourished, the handicapped, standards of living, nutrition, literacy, longevity, etc. In many instances, world conferences and international years have been used to arouse the people's awareness: the UN World Population Conference, the two World Women's Conferences, the World Youth Conference, the World Racism Conferences, the World Assembly on Aging, various economic and social conferences, a World Employment Conference, the International Year of the Child, the International Year of Disabled Persons, etc.

Much less progress has been achieved on the qualitative aspects of the human family. We do not even possess the rudiments of a comprehensive physiology, sociology, psychology or philosophy for the human race as a whole.

Even more troublesome is the fact that little attention has been paid to the reasons why humans associate, assert a group, fight for it, glorify it, place it above other groups, including humanity, seek advantages, belittle and denigrate others. The total cosmos of these social groups is so complex that it seems almost unmanageable. People coalesce in a race, a nation, a language, a religion, a culture, a region, a continent, an alliance, an ideology, a company, a profession and they behave as if that group were the most important one on earth. We have at this moment a multitude of groups founded on old as well as new beliefs, interests and common characteristics. Many of them think that they hold the ultimate truth, that others are wrong and that the rest of the world should accept *their* truth, way of life and beliefs. The sociology of this cosmos has barely retained humanity's attention. I will return to this when trying to determine how "right human relations" can be established and what progress is being made.

The Personal or Individual Cosmos

Finally, the last cosmos which is of importance to you and to me is the personal or individual cosmos, that miracle of temporary consciousness, matter, energy, spirit, mind and heart, linked with the rest of the world and the heavens, but also self-contained, autonomous and well defined, as are all other cosmoses from the infinitely large to the infinitely small.

Regarding the physical aspects of individual life, humanity has made enormous progress. Our material life has improved immensely: food, health, shelter, security, mobility are available to more humans than at any previous period of evolution. Our lives are longer than ever before. Of course, this progress has not yet reached equally all regions of the world, but there is constant progress as is evidenced in the UN agencies and forums concerned with the problems of health, food, nutrition, industry and housing. We have made enormous progress in eradicating major diseases and epidemics, in better understanding the nutrition and functioning of the human body, how it can be improved, lengthened and perhaps someday arrive at near perfection. New problems of course also arise as we change the environment. In the affluent countries, the major killers are now brought about by the new environment: cancer, heart diseases and accidents.

In the realm of the mind, each of us knows more today than any king or emperor in the past. For a few dollars we can buy a paperback describing the universe. Never have there been so many literate people on this planet. The fulfillment of the human person from the point of view of knowledge has been prodigious, to the point that the environment again is moving in on us: too many ideas, too many writings, too much news, too many claims of truth, quality and novelty, a saturation of a complexity which bewilders, creates anxiety and unhappiness, and often drives the individual away from his civilization.

There has been considerably less progress on the moral, sentimental and spiritual planes, although some advances are noticeable on fundamental human rights, world solidarity and altruism, as well as a revival of spirituality. But the science and arts of living have lagged considerably behind, neglecting to explore and develop the immense possibilities offered by the human heart and soul. This transcendence is not even discussed in the world forums. The scientific and industrial revolutions have paid little attention to the fundamental questions: "Why am I on earth? How do I relate to the universe, to creation, to the eternal stream of life and time? What are the meaning and purpose of life? What is the sense of it all?" These philosophical and spiritual questions have not yet reached the United Nations as an institution, but they were power-

fully incarnated in individuals such as Dag Hammarskjöld and
U Thant.

In short, one could say that as a species we have achieved considerable progress in our knowledge and piercing of the surrounding
world; that good progress is being made towards the increased
fulfillment and flowering of the miracle of individual life, especially
in the material and intellectual fields; but that progress is lagging
farthest behind in the political and social spheres. For example,
while the world abounds with religious, moral, ethical and legal
precepts for the behavior and conduct of the individual, there is
barely the beginning of similar ethics for the conduct of institutions,
including the most powerful of all, namely, armed nations. For a private person to kill another human being is a crime. For a nation to
kill wholesale is heroism. Is this situation hopeless? Can we ever
emerge from the sea of contradictions and complexities inherited
and unlocked by ourselves on our strange little planet twirling in the
universe? This is the main challenge of our time and we will need
much optimism, vision and determination to keep civilization on its
upward path.

A Gigantic Biological Process

For science the future is bright: there remains so much to be uncovered and investigated in innumerable fields. For the human
being, progress is needed with regard to interiority, morality and
spirituality, and more generally for the achievement of happiness,
which is the culmination of the miracle of life. But what can be
done with regard to the social cosmos?

In this respect, nobody knows today how the world will look in a
hundred years. Existing groups are protecting themselves, among
other ways, with frightful arms, and are trying to gain ground over
each other in a thousand overt and covert ways. New groups such as
the transnational corporations are being born and progressing rapidly. Is this situation hopeless? Will we ever see decent, harmonious,
happy, peaceful, orderly, satisfying human relations on this planet?
Yes, I think so. Someday it will all work out for the best of the
human race, but we do not know when and how, for this gigantic biological process of adaptation has only begun. In this regard we can
discern a few basic trends and hopeful signs.

The first and fundamental task is to prevent these groups from slaughtering each other and blowing up our planet and life in the process. This is the most immediate priority. The first thing to do at this juncture of evolution, whenever a conflict is about to break out or whenever power—new or old—is beginning to grow excessively, *is to build bridges*. This is one of the fundamental and historical tasks of the United Nations: constantly to build bridges and to let off steam so that tensions and pressures, be they territorial claims, poverty, injustice, inequality, violation of human rights, etc., are prevented from creating havoc. Thus, each year at the end of three months of General Assembly, statesmen and -women have learned something from each other, they have become a little wiser, they better understand the other side's point of view. There is a little more give and take, and as a result, progressively, we are moving closer towards each other in the consideration and understanding of our common fate on planet Earth.

This is the most important task we must perform for the moment and it is taking place in dozens of world agencies and innumerable meetings on practically every conceivable subject, difference and tension. Once the last conflicts have disappeared, the leaders of nations will discover a completely new world in the making, a new age of which they had no idea but which they themselves helped to prepare in the network of international organizations they created. These are becoming a sort of brain, heart, nervous system and soul for the human species. Yes, the UN's first and paramount task is to build bridges, to help avoid the gigantic and murderous conflagrations which could well erupt during the present Promethean period of change.

Another source of hope for the improvement of human relations is the fact that governments and other large entities are beginning to discover that *they cannot win it all* and that within our biosphere, our planet, our solar system and the universe they are after all not so great and powerful. They are beginning to understand that there are innumerable forces at work in the present stage of evolution and that within the framework of our given reality and resources they cannot pursue very far their dreams of total dominion. I have accompanied the Secretary-General on several state visits. Everywhere, leaders of nations considered the environment to be one of the most important problems of our planet. They were right. They knew that this new preoccupation was moving in on us and that it provided them with opportunities to cooperate and put somewhat aside the old ideologies and values inherited from their predecessors and in which they often no longer believe. Ecumenism is a major phenomenon of our time: it is a new philosophy which helps religions to stop hating and fighting each other in the name of God. It will also help nations to stop slaughtering each other in the name of the goddess National Sovereignty. Thus, planetary understanding of the global conditions of human life on earth is one of our greatest chances. The new conditions will change the political scene and political thinking for ages to come. World cooperation has become a powerful asset, brought about by the deep forces which are at work in the present phase of evolution.

It is vitally necessary to take advantage of the period of physical stability of our planet and of stable energy flows from our sun. The current human quarrels and atomic endangering of our planet are totally incomprehensible if we think of our geophysical and astrophysical luck in the universe. It just cannot be that billions of years of evolution should have had as their sole purpose to see an atomic holocaust put an end to all life on our planet!

If Christ Came Back to Earth

There is another area where considerable progress can be made by the peoples themselves, by the individual as an autonomous free-willed cosmos with a profound influence during his lifetime on his family, community, nation, religion or profession: the emergence and advancement of the notion of the *human family*. In the midst of the deafening claims of so many groups, who speaks for the human family as Christ did two thousand years ago? I admit that all races are important, that all nations are important, that all religions are important, that East, West, North and South are important, but what about *humanity as a whole*? What attention, what priority does that supreme family of all receive in our civilization, in the media, in the schools, in literature, in the arts, in churches, in our homes? As for me, after having lived through a horrible war and an uncertain peace, after having seen my own family torn between two nations, I have decided long ago that the only realities that matter for me are God, planet Earth, humanity, my family and myself. All other groups are in constant change: their borders, their priorities, their power, their allegiances change. But God, the planet, humanity, the natural family and the miracle of individual life are permanent realities in our cosmic presence and adventure. We do not do enough for the human family. Therefore, if you are an anthropologist, I would beg you to help develop a science of total human anthropology and study the new global concerns and institutions of the human race. If you are a psychologist, please help develop a science of world psychology. Why do we have a world youth problem simultaneously in most countries? Why are there world scares? Why do people experience a psychological togetherness in world Olympics? Could we not develop world musical and other art festivals? There are so many beautiful and useful things the world's peoples could do together. There *is* a world psychology, because there is a world public opinion, owing to rapid communications. The same is true of world philosophy, world sociology and world spirituality. Where are the philosophers who have the courage to speak out for the whole human race? If Kant were alive today he would come to the United Nations and rewrite his *Project for Perpetual Peace*. If Christ came back to earth, his first visit would be to the United Nations to see if his dream of human oneness and brotherhood had come true. He would be happy to see representatives of all nations, North and South, East and West, rich and poor, believers and nonbelievers, young and old, Philistines and Samaritans, trying to find answers to the perennial questions of human destiny and fulfillment. But how many disappointments and criticisms would he have? Would he not say that, without seeing ourselves as one family and asking ourselves the fundamental questions of life and of our relations with the Creator and the universe, we will never make it?

A World-wide Bimillennium Celebration of Life

I have observed during my lifetime that it is difficult to hold together any human group for long if there is not a vision, an ideal, an objective, a dream. To bind the human family together, to foster its further ascent, to prevent it from losing ground and falling into the abyss of despair, we must have a constant vision, a dream for the human family. We will not swim forever in the present sea of complexity if we are not shown a shore. Unfortunately when one looks at the curricula of schools and universities, at the media and literature, one does not find any shores. The dreams of peace, of world fraternity and of the United Nations are all too often scoffed at and ignored as childish and hopeless fantasies. Of course, they become hopeless by the mere disbelief of the people. Peace and right human relations are not solely matters for governments and international agencies. They are the concern of every human being. There is an immense power for peace and good in the four and a half billion people of this planet. We each have our sphere of influence. No government can forever remain insensitive to the people's demands. The defense of peace, good human relations and the United Nations rests largely in the hands of the people. Nothing prevents them from joining United Nations associations or citizens' groups for peace. Never should one underestimate the real power of the people and of their dreams, if they really want to be heard. This is why, on the occasion of Earth Day, I proposed that humanity should hold in the year 2000 a world-wide Bimillennium Celebration of Life preceded by unparalleled thinking, perception, inspiration, elevation, planning and love for the achievement of a peaceful, happy and godly human society on earth.[1]

Beyond the Imperialism of Reason

I would like to point out another domain where there is good hope for a further ascent in human relations: *the world of the heart.* During the last three hundred years humanity's progress has been essentially of an intellectual and material nature. The imperialism of reason had little room or respect for sentiment. Scientists and thinkers believed that everything could be solved, explained and furthered by means of pure physical manipulation and intellect. We seem to have come to the end of that belief. How many times do we see in the United Nations that world problems are insoluble because of the excessive intelligence of the antagonists? Piles of arguments mount endlessly on each side with no solution in sight. Usually it takes a great statesman to brush it all aside and to decide that he will see his adversary, sit down with him, forget about all arguments and find a peaceful solution simply because he is determined to find one. In diplomatic and political science courses young people are being taught the intricacies of intellectualism and systematic falsehoods: lies are called "negotiating positions" and the truth is called

[1] See Sister Margaret McGurn, I.H.M., "Global Spirituality, Planetary Consciousness in the thought of Teilhard de Chardin and Robert Muller, with a proposal for a Bimillennium Celebration of Life," World Happiness and Cooperation, Ardsley-on-Hudson, 1979.

a "fallback position." With such immorality we will go nowhere. Freud pointed to the right path in his famous reply to Einstein in 1932, when he said that the instinct of aggression in man could only be counteracted by the development of love or sentiment. Hence his recommendation that ties of sentiment or love for the earth, for all its people and for international institutions be developed. He considered the League of Nations to be an experiment without precedent which would call into play certain idealistic attitudes of mind, an identification with the totality of the group, and in the end might hold the world together. What he said then is even truer today.

Humanity has done marvels in the last few hundred years in developing human senses and comprehension through stupendous scientific and technological inventions. This march of knowledge and intelligence will go on, uncovering a heretofore unknown reality which has existed all around us since the beginning of time. But there is no reason for downgrading the heart and the soul. The miracles of science must be repeated now in the fields of sentiment and interiority. Human beings must again be seen as total beings, able to fulfill themselves and to act with the full capacity of the qualities deposited in us by God and evolution. Once this is done, most problems will fall into place and become soluble. In order to see right, to think right and to act right we must visualize our place in the total universe and in time, as all great prophets, spiritual leaders and philosophers have told us since the beginning. We must absolutely restore the great moral forces of love, compassion, truthfulness, optimism and faith in human destiny which have always been at the root of civilization. They alone will enable us to see the light and the great simplicity of the pattern of evolution foreseen by God amidst the complexities, obscurities and anxieties of the present time.

Learning to Live Together

The greatest avenue to right human relations is *education*. The human family is continuously renewed: every hour about 6,000 people die and 15,000 babies are born. All these newcomers must be educated in the perception and art of living, so as to fulfill the miracle of life they have been given. In this chain, our knowledge and wisdom are transmitted constantly at higher levels. Education starts with the mother and in the home, and is later continued in educational institutions. Babies are born with blank minds and then are "wired in" by education and their social environment. It will become increasingly important, if we wish to establish right human relations, to give the children the right universal education. This is probably the most important problem we face on this planet. Children are "wired in" with slanted values and distorted information about our globe, its people, the human destiny and our place in the universe and in time.

We cannot obtain right human relations if we do not give the children an honest view of the world into which they are born. We must give them a global view of the planet's marvels and conditions, of the human family and its rich diversity, we must give them to understand that they are a cosmos of their own endowed with the miracle of life among innumerable brethren and sisters on our planet. We must tell each child that he is a unique happening in the universe which will never be repeated in exactly the same form. Right human relations require that we tell the children how they should relate to the skies, to the stars, to the sun, to the infinite, to time, to the human family, to their planet and to all their human brethren and sisters. We must tell them that they have only a few years to live and that they must think what will become of them after they die. We must tell them a story which no longer has anything to do with idealism but which reflects common facts derived from the collective efforts of the human family to learn, to understand and to elevate itself.

This will require a real revolution in education, which will happen sooner or later. Education is really the key to our future. Former Secretary-General U Thant, who was a teacher, often said to me: "Robert, we are too old to bring about the necessary changes in the world. Only the younger generation can do it. And, for that, education is the key." This was why he supported so strongly international schools and proposed the creation of a United Nations University, which exists today. He dreamed that one university on this planet would give all other universities the global views, inspiration and curricula needed for a peaceful society and right human relations. There is so much prejudice in ourselves. We have constant allegiances and preferences for groups instead of for the total human family. We make absolutes of what should be only relative. It is programed into us, it is "wired in." But bridges and interconnections are being built. We are learning from each other. We are more peaceful than we ever were. We are making constant progress in human relations. We no longer act towards each other like wild, scared animals.

I am convinced that this process of learning will also extend progressively to nations, human groups and institutions. We are entering one of the most fascinating and challenging eras of human evolution. In order to win this great new battle for civilization we must be able to rely upon a vastly increased number of people with a world view. We need world managers and servers in many fields: in the UN and the budding new world institutions, in government, in churches, in world companies, in transnational professional associations. Even if progress at the level of the child may still be distant, owing to the idiosyncrasies of national education, at least at the university level the time has come to make progress and to establish entirely new global curricula aimed at the needs of the new emerging world society.

On the Right Path

I firmly believe that the human race will succeed someday in establishing right human relations and that such a day may not be quite as distant as we think. I come from the border between two countries, France and Germany. I have seen hatred and horrors which I could not have imagined as a child. If someone had told me that peace would someday bless that region and that France and Germany would become friendly towards each other, I would not have believed it. And yet it happened! What was possible between two archenemies like France and Germany can also be possible for the entire world. Humanity has been able to avoid another world war during one of the most dangerous periods ever in its evolution. When I observe the degree of cooperation that already exists at the UN and in the various world agencies, I can only conclude that we are at long last on the right path and that we will find progressively the proper human relations on this planet.

I would even say more: I firmly believe that humanity will be able to elevate human life to unprecedented levels and achieve a happy society on earth. We have this possibility. We have been given by God and evolution the means, the intelligence, the heart and the soul necessary for that. As distinct from other living species, we have the capacity to raise ourselves to higher levels of fulfillment and consciousness. Therefore, in spite of much foolishness, nonsensical armaments and excessive risks of accidents, which ought to be eliminated as quickly as possible, I would unhesitatingly throw down my gauntlet in favor of the success of the human race. The battle of right human relations which started thousands of years ago on this planet will someday be won, and I think rather soon.

3

A Copernican View of World Cooperation

An event which greatly helped me to understand better our global world was a meeting of the American Association of Systems Analysts held in New York City in the 1970s. The organizers had requested that the United Nations send them a speaker on the subject "Can the United Nations become a functional system of world order?"

I was intrigued by the question. What was meant by "functional system of world order"? Who were these men who called themselves "systems analysts"? What was this new science? I was unable to find a speaker among our UN experts, for we simply did not have any systems analysts. Remembering the severe words of H. G. Wells directed at the League of Nations,[1] I decided to go and speak to the congress myself. I attended the meeting during a weekend, which gave me an opportunity to listen to the other speakers and to get acquainted with them. They were very remarkable people—philosophers, sociologists, biologists, mathematicians—who were trying to devise a new world order from the immensely complex relations which bind everything together on our earth. They were the new scientists of interdependence. I was at a loss, however, as to what I could say to them. Their science was too complex, too math-

[1] "Does this League of Nations contain within it the germ of any permanent federation of human effort? Will it grow into something for which men will be ready to work whole-heartedly and, if necessary, fight—as hitherto they have been willing to fight for their country and their own people? There are few intimations of any such enthusiasm for the League at the present time. The League does not even seem to know how to talk to the common men. It has gone into official buildings and comparatively few people in the world understand or care what it is doing there." Wells, *Outline of History* (London: The Macmillan Company, 1920), Vol. II, Book IX, pp. 583–84.

ematical for me. I did not know the first rudiments of it. To pretend the contrary would have been foolish. Nevertheless, I had to answer as well as possible a very simple question. "Does the United Nations perform functions which contribute to the peace, order, justice, well-being and happiness of humans on this planet?"

Since the listeners were experts in "systems," the least I could do was to present the UN's work in a "systematic" way. I tried to conceive the most general framework possible. I visualized therefore our globe hanging in the universe and saw it first in its relations with the sun. I viewed it then as an orange cut in half and saw its atmosphere, its crust and its thin layer of life or biosphere. Within the biosphere, I saw the seas, the oceans, the polar caps, the continents, the mountains, the rivers, the lakes, the soils, the deserts, the animals, the plants and the humans. Within the crust of the earth I saw the depths of the oceans, the continental plates, the underground reservoirs of water, oil, minerals and heat. Within the mass of several billion people, I saw the nations, races, religions, cultures, languages, cities, industries, farms, professions, corporations, institutions, armies, families, down to that incredible cosmos, the human being. In the human person, I saw the rich, miraculous system of body, mind, heart and spirit linked through senses with the heavens and the earth. I visualized that person from conception to death. I saw the sixty trillion cells of his body, the infinitely small, the atom, microbial life, the incredible world of genes, which embody and transmit the patterns of life. And all along this Copernican path, at each step, I asked myself the question: "Are humans cooperating on this subject? Are they trying to understand it, to appraise it, to see it in relation to everything else and to determine what is good or bad for humans, what should be changed or not? Was the subject before the United Nations or one of its agencies? Was the United Nations 'system' dealing with it?" And the answer was usually yes.

Yes, the UN is dealing with the relations between our planet and its sun: in 1954 UNESCO convened a first colloquium on solar energy; in 1961 the UN convened a world conference on new forms of energy and produced three volumes on solar energy; in 1973, UNESCO sponsored an international conference on "The Sun in the Service of Mankind" which reviewed all relations between our star and ourselves—energy, food, climate, life and habitat. And in 1981 the UN held a second world conference on new and renewable sources of energy, including the sun.

Yes, the UN is dealing with outer space: a treaty on outer space was concluded in 1967 and a world conference was held on this new frontier in 1968; outer space has been declared a common heritage of humankind, free of all weapons; objects launched into space are registered with the UN; astronauts are envoys of humanity; damages caused by objects falling from space are regulated by a UN convention; a treaty on the moon and other celestial bodies has been adopted; the International Telecommunication Union allocates frequency bands for satellite telecommunications; the World Meteorological Organization receives world-wide weather and climate data from satellites; the International Maritime Organization has an international satellite which serves all ships and navigators around the world; the Food and Agriculture Organization receives outer space information on weather, crop outlooks, floods and plant epidemics; UNESCO is testing educational systems by means of satellites, and the UN held another outer space conference in 1982.

Yes, the UN is dealing with the gaseous layer surrounding our globe, the atmosphere with its components, the troposphere, stratosphere and ionosphere. Under the auspices of the World Meteorological Organization, governments are cooperating in a Global Atmospheric Research Program. The United Nations Environment Program (UNEP) is keeping a check on the state and the quality of the atmosphere and the ionosphere. It convened in 1978 a world conference on the ozonosphere. The International Civil Aviation Organization is dealing with air safety, international air traffic and a legal order for world air transport.

Yes, the UN is concerned with our globe's climate, including the possible recurrence of ice ages: the World Meteorological Organization held a first world climate conference in 1979.

Yes, the UN is concerned with the total biosphere through project Earthwatch, the Global Environment Program of UNEP and UNESCO's program, "Man and the Biosphere."

Yes, the UN is dealing with our planet's seas and oceans through the Law of the Sea Conference, UNESCO's Intergovernmental Oceanographic Commission, FAO's work on world fisheries, IMCO's concern with maritime transport, UNEP's work and treaties on the sea environment, etc.

Yes, the UN is dealing with the world's deserts through FAO, UNESCO and UNEP. A world conference on desertification was held in 1977.

Yes, the UN is dealing with the world's water resources and cycles: UNESCO has a World Hydrological Decade, the UN held a world water conference in 1978 and established a map of our globe's underground water resources.

Yes, the UN is dealing with the continental plates, international rivers, underdeveloped nations, the cultures, races, religions, languages, cities, infants, adolescents, women, malnourished, workers, farmers, professionals, corporations and almost any other conceivable group or global problem of this planet.

Yes, the UN is dealing with the human person, that alpha and omega of our efforts, the basic unit of all this gigantic Copernican tapestry. The person's basic rights, justice, health, progress and peace are being dealt with from the fetus to the time of death.

Yes, the UN is dealing with the atom in the International Atomic Energy Agency, and with microbiology and genetics in UNESCO, the World Health Organization and FAO.

Yes, the UN is dealing with art, folklore, nature, the preservation of species, germ banks, labor, handicrafts, literature, industry, trade, tourism, energy, finance, birth defects, sicknesses, pollution, politics, the prevention of accidents, of war and conflicts, the building of peace, the eradication of armaments, atomic radiation, the settlement of disputes, the development of world-wide cooperation, the aspirations of East and West, North and South, black and white, rich and poor, etc.

I went on like this for more than an hour. When I finished, I still had a bagful to say, but I was exhausted by my exaltation at the vastness of the cooperation I had seen develop over my thirty years of service in the United Nations.[2] It was now very clear to me: there was a pattern in all this; it was a response to a prodigious evolutionary march by the human species towards total consciousness, an attempt by man to become the all-understanding, all-enlightened, all-embracing master of his planet and of his being. Something gigantic was going on, a real turning point in evolution, the beginning of an entirely new era of which international cooperation at the UN was only a first outward reflection. I had not seen it so far, because it had come in a haphazard way, in response to specific events, needs, crises and perceptions by governments and individuals all over the planet. But the result was now clearly here, glorious and beautiful

[2] See Appendix at end of chapter.

like Aphrodite emerging from the sea. This was the beginning of a new age, a gigantic step forward in evolution. It was unprecedented and full of immense hope for humanity's future on this planet. Perhaps after all we would be able to achieve peace and harmony on earth. This time, humankind would be forced to think out absolutely everything and to measure the totality of our planet's conditions and evolution in our solar system and in time. The games of glory, aggrandizement and domination by specific groups would soon come to an end. The great hour of truth had arrived for the human race.

I saw it all coming ever more forcefully, despite the disbeliefs and grins of the cynics. What was the sense of it all? It was simply to achieve peace, justice, order and progress for everybody. And what was behind peace, justice, order and progress? The attainment of happiness and of an unprecedented consciousness and fulfillment of all guests admitted to the miracle of life!

When I finished, there was a long silence in the audience. No one applauded for a while. What I had said was probably too farfetched, too exalted, too beautiful to be true. Or perhaps each listener was absorbed in his own thoughts and perceptions of the incredible human adventure on our fabulous little planet spinning in the universe. At last one of the panel members, a biologist, Edgar Taschdjian, broke the silence and said:

"Friends, I had heard several proposals for world systems during our Congress. Their authors thought that they had embraced the entire world. But I had told you that the most daring of them did not reach the heel of what existed already in the United Nations. I am sure that Mr. Muller would be at a loss to provide us with a complete chart of all the agencies, programs, organs, suborgans, centers, groups, meetings, arrangements and consortia which compose today the United Nations system. Anyway, this system is changing so fast that a static presentation of it would be of little value. Yes, my friends, we are far behind the actual, political world. We must awaken to this fact and raise our sight to the height already attained by the United Nations system. . . ."

I was thinking at high speed during that time: in my Copernican overview I had found several gaps; there was no world-wide cooperation for the globe's cold zones, the mountains, our topsoil, standardization, world safety, prevention, the family, morality, spirituality, world psychology and sociology, the world of the senses, the inner realm of the individual, his needs, values, perceptions, love and happiness. Cooperation was insufficient on consumer protection,[3] on the world's 450 million handicapped, on the world's elderly,[4] on world law, on the ultimate meaning of human life and its objectives. And political men were still dragging their feet in antiquated, obsolete quarrels which prevented them from seeing the vast new universal scheme of evolution which was dawning upon the world.

Or was I dreaming and living in a sphere of fantasy and wishful thinking, like Teilhard de Chardin, H. G. Wells, Albert Schweitzer, Sri Aurobindo, Sri Chinmoy and a growing number of others? They too saw the world from the outside, as it hangs and twirls in the universe, and had visualized the grand journey of humanity towards oneness, convergence and unprecedented happiness. Were they all wrong? Was I wrong too? No. Everything I had learned, lived and observed pragmatically day by day for thirty years in the UN realistically pointed to it. We were approaching Teilhard's point of convergence, Wells's last chapter of *The Outline of History*, Schweitzer's reverence for life, Sri Aurobindo's total consciousness, Sri Chinmoy's world oneness. It was coming as a political reality and much faster than anyone could dare to hope. For the first time in human evolution, it came as a world-wide wave, above and beyond all disciplines and groups, born from our knowledge of the wonders and limits of our planet. And it was only the mere beginning of the apotheosis of human life on earth. Still there was missing a great core of political humanists, thinkers, prophets, poets and leaders of people who would concern themselves with the deeper objectives and reasons of human life, its uniqueness, its miraculous character, our full potentials, our perceptions, sentiments and inner lives. But they would come soon. What a prodigious time we are about to live!

Suddenly an image came to my mind. It was the good person of U Thant. He too had foreseen a serene, enlightened world, a world of peace and understanding enriched by ethics, morality, love, spirituality and philosophy. I remembered the scene at a reception he had offered to the U.S. astronauts after the first moon landing. I was talking in a corner with one of the astronauts. The Secretary-

[3] This subject has now been taken up by the Economic and Social Council.
[4] This has been corrected: 1981 has been proclaimed International Year of Disabled Persons, and a world conference on aging was held in 1982.

General came near us and inquired what we were talking about. The astronaut answered:

"Your colleague is asking me what I thought when I saw for the first time the entire earth from outer space."

"Oh, I see!" said U Thant. "I am not surprised by his question. But I am afraid he is not expecting anything new from you. He just wants a confirmation, for he has been living on the moon long before you, looking down on earth with his global eyes, trying to figure out what the human destiny will be."

Vanity of vanities! U Thant was reminding me to take all this with a grain of salt and to return to earth! My Copernican scheme receded for a moment from my mind and there remained only his enigmatic and kind smile, while the systems analysts were pursuing a discussion which became more and more incomprehensible to me. . . .

APPENDIX

The mere list of the eighteen United Nations specialized agencies and fourteen world programs which compose the UN system illustrates the vastness of today's international cooperation. No other living species has ever so equipped itself with global instruments designed to study, observe, monitor and preserve its habitat. In innumerable organs, meetings and conferences, through thousands of experts and delegates, backed by forty thousand world servants, humankind is today probing its entire biosphere and condition, trying to augment peace, to reduce conflicts and tensions, to build bridges and to seek ways for a greater fulfillment of human life to an extent which no philosopher, prophet or social reformer would have ever dreamed possible.

Here is a quick overview of this incipient world system: The eighteen *specialized agencies*: International Atomic Energy Agency (IAEA); International Labor Organization (ILO); Food and Agriculture Organization (FAO); United Nations Educational, Scientific and Cultural Organization (UNESCO); World Health Organization (WHO); International Bank for Reconstruction and Development (IBRD); International Development Association (IDA); International Finance Corporation (IFC); International Monetary Fund (IMF); International Civil Aviation Organization (ICAO); Universal Postal Union (UPU); International Telecommunication Union

(ITU); World Meteorological Organization (WMO); International Maritime Organization (IMO); General Agreement on Tariffs and Trade (GATT); World Intellectual Property Organization (WIPO); International Fund for Agricultural Development (IFAD); World Tourism Organization (WTO), linked with the UN under a novel type of agreement.

The fourteen *special programs:* United Nations Children's Fund (UNICEF); United Nations Conference on Trade and Development (UNCTAD); United Nations Development Program (UNDP); Office of UN Disaster Relief Co-ordinator (UNDRO); United Nations Environment Program (UNEP); United Nations Fund for Drug Abuse Control (UNFDAC); Office of the United Nations High Commissioner for Refugees (UNHCR); United Nations Industrial Development Organization (UNIDO); United Nations Institute for Training and Research (UNITAR); United Nations Fund for Population Activities (UNFPA); United Nations Relief and Works Agency (UNRWA); United Nations University (UNU); United Nations Volunteers (UNV); World Food Program (WFP).

The UN itself is concerned with a multitude of global problems, such as peace, disarmament, outer space, the seas and oceans, natural resources, human rights, racial equality, women, multinational corporations, criminality, etc.

There also exists a first world ministerial council: the World Food Council. Hopefully, similar councils will be established in other crucial fields, energy in particular.

4

Towards a New Spiritual Ideology

It strikes us vividly that the very life and perceptions of the human race are deeply entrenched in our terrestrial environment. We are living beings born, developing and seeking fulfillment in specific planetary conditions: a given atmosphere, a given crust to stand on, a given warmth due to our distance from the sun, a given absorption of the sun's energy by plants and animals. In the entire universe there is probably no other planet offering the same conditions and evolution.

One of the first fundamental elements of that environment which must have struck early humans indelibly is the result of the rotation and orbit of the earth, that is, the succession of day and night, light and darkness, warmth and cold, the change in seasons, the birth and death of nature. Human life on our planet was therefore basically influenced from the beginning by a duality, a constant switch on and off, back and forth, a view of everything from a light or dark side, a mood of optimism or pessimism, hope or despair, life affirmation or fear of death, faith or abandonment.

This dual mechanism "wired into" us by our planet's rotation was reinforced by the life process itself. The learning of life by each newborn individual is indeed a road of trial and error, of finding what is "right" and "wrong," be it in movements, foods, actions, thoughts, beliefs or sentiments. The history of our civilization is the sum total of this learning process by peoples all over the planet, through trials and errors, transmitted from generation to generation in oral and recorded ways. What was found to be good for human life was retained and what was bad was rejected. Since humans were scattered over the earth and were living in different natural environments without much communication with each other, different cultures and civilizations developed which have both common and distinctive characteristics: we all eat, drink, talk, love, create and believe; but we eat a vast variety of foods, use five thousand languages, have many different forms of art and believe in many different faiths and social systems.

One of the most fundamental events of our own time is the convergence of all these life experiences and civilizations and the extraction therefrom of common denominators of what is good or bad for the entire human race. It is the great question of unity in diversity, complicated by the natural tendency of each group, culture, language, way of life, religion and social system to believe that it is the best in the world and that others would be well advised to follow it. Some of them might be very aggressive and expansionist, while others are simply on the defensive in order to survive and escape destruction. This is what causes the immense complexity of today's political, social, religious and cultural scene. Humanity is torn between diverse identities on the one hand and strong currents towards greater unity on the other, and we are only at the beginning of finding out what is "good" or "bad" for humankind as a whole.

There is another reason why the problem of good or bad is so complicated today. During the past few hundred years, and especially since the last world war, we have extended tremendously our physical and mental awareness of our planet by means of science and technology. As a result, we have uncovered an immensely complex reality, which always existed around us but most of which had remained hidden to our senses. Hence the bewildering number of new problems unlocked by our own discoveries and physical transformations of the planet. For example, are the thousands of new chemicals invented and produced every year good or bad for the intake of our bodies? Are new ideas, beliefs, writings, media, communications and advertising good or bad for the intake of our minds? Are faster methods of transportation good or bad? And so forth. We have steadfastly believed for centuries in new discoveries, in changing our conditions, in new industries and economic development, and suddenly there appear serious question marks: should we continue to change our planet at all? If we change it at the present rate, what will it look like and how will human life fare in a future which astrophysicists estimate to be between six and eight billion years?

So, while there is immense progress at the present time in extending human knowledge and mastery in every conceivable direction, there are also vast interrogations, accompanied by deep anxiety. What must we do under these circumstances? First and foremost we must emerge successfully from the shock of the bewildering complexities engendered by scientific discovery and growing human activity: we must put order in our knowledge and derive therefrom a correct image of our place in the universe and in time. As on the eve of the French Revolution, we need a right encyclopedia. Secondly, we must now deliberately take full cognizance of our given planetary environment and realize that we are living in one self-contained, interdependent, highly complex and fragile planetary system. Thirdly, we must outgrow the increasingly erroneous notion of good and bad as seen by a particular group, be it a race, a nation, a faith, an ideology or a business, and define new concepts of what is good or bad for the entire human family. This is absolutely essential. The recent discovery of the interdependent wholeness of our planet must be accompanied by the recognition of the interdependent wholeness of humanity.

For the first time in history, the question of the survival of the entire human family, rather than that of any particular nation or group, has been squarely posed. Many scientists who deal with the long run do not give us much chance of survival. Some do not think that the human species will survive for another ten thousand years, a mere speck in time. They believe that human intelligence, which was a compensation for our species' lack of physical strength, will now lead to our self-destruction. Others, on the contrary, believe that humanity is undergoing a deep evolutionary change and will develop new means and perceptions which will help it survive and find a harmonious relation with its planet and with its own individuals. Having seen the birth of several world-wide organs of diagnosis, monitoring, warning and collective action in the United Nations, I place myself unhesitatingly in that second group.

Finally, in the prodigious process which lies ahead of us, we must restore optimism and continue to sharpen our inborn instincts for life, for the positive, for self-preservation, for survival and human fulfillment at ever higher levels of consciousness. We must conquer the duality, the somber, the bad, the negative, the suicidal. These all contain dangerous self-feeding processes of destruction. We must turn instead to the mysterious self-generating powers of hope, creative thinking, love, life affirmation and faith as they were taught to us by Christ and by all great religious leaders.

The cosmos of the human family is not very different from the individual human person. Each of us is an immensely complex unit, and within each of us every little cell is an immensely complex cosmos of its own. The trillions of cells and many automatic processes of our being are held together and made to function harmoniously through the guiding principle of life itself: if we are optimistic, positive, hopeful, happy to be alive, all is well—the myriads of little factories will all work together in harmony, spurned by higher, elevating forces. If, on the contrary, we give up, let go, despair, then sickness, malfunctioning and often death will occur. It cannot be otherwise. In all living beings there must be foremost a will for life. The greatest freedom of the human being is his choice to believe in life and in himself and thus to be fully part of the eternal stream of creation and evolution. We do not always pay sufficient attention to this fundamental two-way mechanism in the human person and in social bodies, this "night and day" complex inherent in our planetary conditions.

It is the fundamental task of education to teach all new members of the human family to give optimistic guidance to their miraculous bodies, minds, hearts and souls in the complexity of our stupendous reality. Such self-awakening must take place within a peaceful, total human society also guided by belief in our miraculous, luminous journey on an incredible planet in the unfathomable universe. All major religions have understood that when they speak of the "miracle of faith."

It is not the first time that humans have been confronted with a bewildering complexity. For primitive man the surrounding awesome and hostile world—the sky, the stars, the sun, lightning, thunder and winter—was at least as frightening as the complexities of today. The human eye receives at every moment more than one hundred million bits of information and yet the optical ganglia, the brain and the heart reduce this baffling complexity to simple notions and objects, to feelings of bad or good, useful or harmful, ugly or beautiful. Humans will always find new simple means and syntheses to help them surmount any conceivable complexity, including the current one. The most urgent need today is to restore the magic powers of love, confidence and belief in the further ascent and perfectibility of humankind.

For the first time in evolution, the human species has assumed a collective responsibility for the success of planet Earth in the universe. Interdependence, globality and a total view of our planet and the environment are now facts of life. But much more is needed: we humans are also entrenched in a universal environment, the cosmos, the total creation and flow of time. We must feel part of all space and time, of the greatness and wonders of the universe. You know and love your home, don't you? Well, you must also know and love your planetary home as well as your universal home, from the infinitely large to the infinitely small. We must stand in awe before the beauty and miracle of creation. Perhaps this will be the new spiritual ideology which will bind the human race. We must lift again our spirits and hearts into the infinite bliss and mystery of the universe. We are too heavy, too earthbound. We must elevate ourselves again as light, cosmic beings in deep communion with the universe and eternity. We must re-establish the unity of our planet and of our beings with the universe and divinity. We must have our roots in the earth and our hearts in heaven. We must see our planet and ourselves as cells of a universe which is becoming increasingly conscious of itself in us. That is our royal road out of the present bewilderment.

5

A Cosmic-Spiritual View

I have been privileged to work for the United Nations almost since its beginning. As I saw the world organization grow and change over the years, I often wondered what the ultimate destination, the end of the journey, would be. Since its birth the United Nations has grown tremendously in scope and in complexity. It encompasses today virtually all nations, thus fulfilling the dream for human universality of many enlightened philosophers, prophets and thinkers. It has branched out into a variety of specialized agencies and world programs concerned with almost every conceivable facet of our planet and of humanity. The process never ends.

I try very hard to understand what this all means in the total stream of time. Are we carried forward, half knowingly, half instinctively, by the will of God or of other forces towards some ultimate objective? What is that objective? What will the image of the world and of its organization be in a hundred, in a thousand years? In my particular function, whence I can see the totality of the world's problems, I could easily drown in an ocean of complexity and despair if I did not detect a logic, a necessity, a sense, an order in all that is happening. Humans were always faced with a very complex reality: our planet is the most complex one in our solar system and we are the most complex species on it. How could our marriage therefore be anything but complex? For our cave-inhabiting forefathers, nature and life were at least as mysterious and complex as they are for us today, but certain great simplifying means were given to us in order to survive and thrive in the maze. The heroic, astounding notions of God, love, peace, beauty, good, happiness and faith came to our rescue and helped us believe and enjoy the great gift of life on our miraculous planet in the immense, mysterious universe.

Today, the known, uncovered reality is a billion times more complex than it was for our forebears. We know so much more about the universe, the infinitely large and outer space, and we have penetrated ever deeper into the infinitely small, the atom and its particles. For example, scientists are wondering these days how nature is able to "package" into a few microns genetic codes, the formulas of which are several feet long! Complete universes and living factories of immense complexity are unceasingly created by nature within astoundingly small spaces. The totality of scientific knowledge is today so minute, so vast and so staggering that many people give up the effort to understand. All this knowledge culminates in the United Nations, nowadays the most complex organization on earth.

And this is far from all: in addition to scientific complexity, we are also the receptacle of all social, man-made and cultural complexities: problems between the North and the South, the East and the West, the rich and the poor, regions, races, sexes, nations, occupations, languages, institutions, firms, etc. No wonder then that the UN has become the social laboratory of our earth, the vastest anthropological institute and political crucible there ever was. It has come to a point where it is well-nigh impossible to draw a complete accurate chart of the whole United Nations system and of its innumerable organs. Strangely enough, such a chart would begin to look like a brain—the brain of the human species.

There must be a sense in all this, a clarity, a heart, a bloodstream, a great human aspiration and creative motion. It is not by accident that all this is happening. There must be a law, a will, a structure in it. It is part of destiny, of our perennial forward march towards fuller, happier and godlier lives for all. It is part of our progressive settling down in our planetary home in the universe. It is part of the fulfillment of increasingly apparent cosmic laws.

I tried to find a scheme, an outline, a table of contents for this fabulous human saga which had to fit in one way or another into my mind.

First, I adopted a classification of all our knowledge from the infinitely large to the infinitely small as it had revealed itself to me during my work at the United Nations: the universe, astrophysics, the solar system, the earth's relations with our sun, outer space, the atmosphere, the biosphere, the continents, the seas and oceans, the mountains, the rivers, the poles, the tropics and equator, the deserts, the earth's crust, the fauna, the flora, the underground sources of water, heat and minerals, down to the microbial world, the genes and the atom. To that cosmic picture of the physical world I added the view of our social cosmos with its innumerable groups, institutions and associations down to the natural family and the individual. For each of these layers of the total physical and human reality I had observed a form of international cooperation somewhere in the United Nations. World cooperation suddenly appeared to me as a prodigious, all-embracing global effort at understanding total reality! What was happening was indeed a progressive falling into place of all scattered, dispersed, uncoordinated human knowledge and efforts all over the planet and over eons of time! As a matter of fact, it is from the United Nations' living world cooperation that my thirst for logic and light was able to discern the cosmic scheme of realities which now presses itself more and more clearly upon us. This was the first facet of the United Nations' cosmic vision.

I had also noticed that humanity was moving increasingly and simultaneously towards a better understanding of our place in time. More and more I saw the United Nations and its agencies concerned with the past: preservation of our elements, of our natural and cultural heritage, of endangered fauna and flora, of genetic material, of antiquities, great landmarks, languages, legends, customs, traditions. Our planet's past evolution and history became ever more precious, as if the human species knew that some losses might impoverish it forever. Simultaneously our concern with the future increased tremendously: there is not a single United Nations agency or program today that does not have at least the year 2000 as its yardstick.

From the infinitely large to the infinitely small, and from the distant past to the unfathomable future, these are the two poles of infinites along which human progress unfolds right under our eyes! It all makes good sense. At our point of evolution, after having groped, tried, erred and learned so much, it is normal that our knowledge should suddenly accelerate and fall into perfect space and time dimensions which always existed and are now becoming increasingly clear to us.

Of course, this mushrooming of knowledge into the four infinites happens to be one of the main causes of our current anxiety. How can we make sense of it? Whom should we believe? What is relevant and useful in all this knowledge? What will our future be? How should we behave? What does life mean in such a universe? What is in it for the individual?

It was U Thant who gave me the key to it. As a Buddhist he believed that humans would never be able to comprehend the total creation and would forever be condemned to live in mystery and "darkness." But he placed the human person at the center of all pre-occupations, the ultimate question being the proper relation between the individual and the surrounding world and universe. Starting, consequently, from the individual, he persistently used and never retreated from a classification of basic human characteristics and needs into physical, intellectual, moral and spiritual. What I had observed at the United Nations bore him out and again made good sense: the paramount importance attached to individual human rights, better nourishment, health, shelter, education, peace, non-violence, compassion, help, cooperation, the many programs in these fields—all this was the story of the physical, mental and moral fulfillment of individual human life. And this effort was now world-wide, with priority attached to the largest discrepancies and most crying injustices. The Universal Declaration of Human Rights was a new magnificent consecration of the individual, and the United Nations Charter was a first code of behavior for nations.

But there was an element missing and it happened to be the one to which U Thant attached the greatest importance: spirituality. He kept repeating that this was the highest and ultimate fulfillment of the human person. How did he define spirituality? For him it was the harmony between the innermost life and the outer life, or the life of the world and the universe. It was a serene comprehension of life in time and in space, the tuning of the inner person with the great mysteries and secrets around him. It was a belief in the goodness of life and the possibility for each human person to contribute his goodness to it. It was the belief in life as part of the eternal stream of time, that each of us came from somewhere and was destined to somewhere, that without such belief there could be no prayer, no meditation, no peace, no happiness. His belief in the long-term improvement of humanity through right individual behavior gave me the last missing piece of the puzzle. Now the universe, our earth and the individual's place in time and in space made sense. What lessons I had received from the United Nations!

Of course I could not fail to notice that this outcome resembled strangely the visions of all great religions. Even without knowing that the world was round, the great prophets and founders of religions had visions which reached from the infinitely small to the infinitely large and from creation to the apocalypse. The Hindu view of the world and trinity, for example, is fully borne out today by the findings of astrophysicists regarding the birth, the stability and the death of a star or solar system. Each religion again saw the fundamental place of the individual human person in the total reality and considered him as a miraculous entity of divine origin, made of physical, mental, moral and spiritual aspirations. Human fulfillment was never limited to purely material and mental progress as it is so often today. Life was to be also a moral achievement and above all a spiritual transcendence. Religions never shied away from the ultimate, fundamental questions: What is life? Why am I on this earth? What is this strange miracle? What is the sense and purpose of it all? What exactly was I given when I was born and admitted to being, to existing? For what and to whom must I be grateful? What should I do, think, feel and hope for? What does my short-lived but so magnificent spark of consciousness mean in the universe?

Spirituality starts with these questions. This is why U Thant gave it the highest value: it represented in his eyes the deepest questions. The answers, of course, have varied greatly during human history: thousands of religions, (with or without God or gods, e.g., Buddhism, Jainism and Sikhism), philosophies and spiritual practices have offered humans their manifold insights and beliefs. Most of them thought that they had the ultimate, total truth or universal principle, and they were all too often prone to fight each other to assert their belief.

So we find that the United Nations is repeating the same old, all-encompassing story. It is forced to it by the nature of things. Year after year, governments increase the scope of the United Nations' work and improve through it their perception of the total reality. This is one of the most prodigious and amazing stories the earth has ever seen. Alas, it is understood by only a very few. But there are two fundamental differences with the past: first, the UN and every nation must integrate the achievements of science and technology within a broader moral and spiritual dimension; and second, while most religions were born in localized, different regions and cultures, this time the story comes from a center, from the place of convergence of all human problems, dreams, aspirations and exertions. The United Nations is the school where they all learn from each other, listen to each other, try to find solutions and define what is good and bad for the whole human race. It is the place of a thousand bridges, the cradle of future world destiny, a lighthouse from which one global signal after the other is emitted to humans all over the globe. It is the birthplace of unique world efforts which help humanity to know itself better and guide its behavior in our planetary home. As Martin Luther King said, "The UN is a gesture in the direction of non-violence on a world scale."

But the religions and the prophets, the poets and the artists did not need a United Nations, a world organization, conferences or experts to help them discover the truth. They saw it straight with their hearts, with an internal vision, with an instinct that went right to the core without getting lost in the convolutions of the mind. They all gave us generally correct codes of conduct, codes of internal serenity, codes of happiness, codes for the highest fulfillment of the miracle of life.

This is why we must listen attentively with all our minds, hearts and souls to what the great religions and spiritual leaders have to say. They have a long experience of human life and often their perceptions are still the quickest and most accurate. This is why we must also be grateful to anyone who gives the work of the United Nations a spiritual interpretation, thus following the examples of Dag Hammarskjöld and U Thant, who saw in the United Nations the renewed story of the total dimension of human life. Their message was one of love, compassion, understanding and human fraternity. That message, after many vicissitudes throughout world history, is re-emerging as forcefully as ever, but now on a universal scale. It is a fascinating story and we are probably the first species ever able to comprehend it. I have always been an optimist, deeply in love with humanity, precisely because of its capacity to elevate and transcend itself into constantly higher levels of physical, intellectual, moral and spiritual fulfillment. The march towards that transcendence has now started on a planetary scale, and we are privileged to be among its first witnesses and workers. We must cater to it, nurture it, love it, help it grow in beauty and in strength, so as to fulfill the prophecies of all great spiritual leaders. In particular I would agree with the prophecy of that spiritual believer in the United Nations, Sri Chinmoy, when he said:

"At the end of its voyage, there is every possibility that the United Nations will be the last word in human perfection. And then the United Nations can easily bloom in excellence and stand as the pinnacle of divine enlightenment."[1]

[1] Sri Chinmoy, "The Inner Message of the United Nations," Dag Hammarskjöld Lecture Series, January 1973.

6

Prayer and Meditation at the United Nations

Prayer, meditation and spirituality at the UN are fascinating subjects. All major world religions are accredited to the United Nations as non-governmental organizations. For example, no less than twenty-four Catholic organizations are represented at the UN. Several of the world's religious leaders have visited the international organization. Most memorable were the visits of His Holiness Pope Paul VI during the General Assembly in 1965 and of Pope John Paul II in 1979. Many religions have special invocations, prayers, hymns and services for the United Nations. The most important examples are those of the Catholic, the Unitarian-Universalist, the Baptist and the Bahai faiths. It is a common practice of the Unitarian-Universalists to display the United Nations flag in their houses of worship. So does the Holy Family Church, the parish church of the UN, with its international reliquary and its many religious services and activities catering to world peace and to the international community.

When it comes to the United Nations proper, one can obviously not say that it is a spiritual organization. How could it be otherwise? For the UN is the creation and mirror of governments, most of whom have "secularized" themselves, i.e., separated spirituality from their daily lives and preoccupations. Nevertheless, prayer and spirituality play an important role in the United Nations. It is a moving experience, for example, to witness the minute of silence for prayer or meditation at the opening of the yearly General Assembly, when men and women from all nations center their minds and souls on the job to be done and when at the end of the Assembly a similar minute of silence permits them to reflect on their achievements and failures.[1] Thus, the world's first universal gatherings of nations are placed under the symbol of prayer or meditation. Also, there are many delegates and world servants whose cultures do not make any distinction between spirituality and public service. Then there are those who are deeply attached to their faiths or for whom the United Nations is a new form of spirituality and ethics, while they remain faithful to their respective religions. Some delegates are known to meditate in a place of worship before speaking in a UN assembly. One of the greatest orators ever at the United Nations, Professor Belaunde from Peru, meditated on his speeches in St. Patrick Cathedral. Then we have the UN Meditation Room, which is visited by hundreds of thousands of visitors each year.[2] We have also a UN Meditation Group led by an Indian mystic. One could tell several moving stories of the spiritual transformation the UN has caused, to the point that this little speck on earth is becoming a holy ground. For example, the rational, intellectual economist Dag Hammarskjöld found God at the United Nations and inspiration for his work as a world servant in the mystics of the Middle Ages. Towards the end, his *Markings* overflow with spirituality and mysticism.

Then there was U Thant, the man from the Orient, who saw no difference between life and religion, who held that spirituality was the highest of all human needs and virtues. The Western distinction between secular and spiritual lives was totally incomprehensible to him. He found in such cleavage one of the principal causes of the world's conflicts, tensions, injustices and disarray. For him, every single moment of life called for prayer, virtue, reverence, gratitude and total communion with humankind and the universe. He was of Buddhist faith, a religion which does not believe in God, and yet he was one of the most spiritual persons I have ever known.

There are many also in the United Nations for whom the cooperation of all nations towards common goals and values is a kind of

[1] Rule 62 of the *Rules of Procedure of the General Assembly* provides: "Immediately after the opening of the first plenary meeting and immediately preceding the closing of the final plenary meeting of each session of the General Assembly, the President shall invite the representatives to observe one minute of silence dedicated to prayer or meditation."

[2] It is symbolic that the new Secretary-General, Mr. Javier Perez de Cuellar, on the first day of his term in January, 1982, visited the UN Meditation Room before proceeding to his office.

new religion, a supreme path or way. They see in the UN the same perennial human dream which has obsessed all great religions and philosophies, namely, the establishment of a peaceful, just, happy, harmonious world society. But there is one difference: while in the past all religions and philosophies were born within specific local, cultural contexts, today we are witnessing the birth of a new philosophy, ideology or ethics which originates from a central place of synthesis where all dreams, aspirations, claims and values of humankind converge. This is new. It constitutes one of the greatest and most exciting attempts at total human fulfillment in the entire evolution of the human race. There has never been anything like it. It is a magnificent story, the beginning of a profound world-wide transformation and transcendence of the human society, a new paradigm of the coming age. True enough, it is as yet a fragile and incomplete story, for the UN largely reflects the priorities and dominant values of our time. For the poorer countries these are food, health, shelter and education, without which there can be no decent life. First one must live, then one can philosophize. In the Western countries too, material, scientific, technological and intellectual achievements generally still occupy the highest priority. They live in an age of rationalism which believes that everything can be explained by scientific, rational means, and this is reflected in the United Nations. But increasingly there are voices which point to other values. U Thant, in particular, was the first great prophet who reminded us of the moral and spiritual dimensions of life and who firmly advocated the development of our moral and spiritual values in order to catch up with rapid technological and scientific advances. For him, the solution of many of our individual, national and international problems rested in the practice of truthfulness, integrity, tolerance, love and brotherhood. And beyond these moral virtues he felt that each individual carried in himself a fundamental question regarding our relationship with the universe and eternity. Hence the paramount place he accorded to spirituality. In his memoirs he wanted to show how spirituality and philosophy should lead, inspire and guide politics.

This point has not yet been reached in the United Nations, but year after year one can observe how moral and ethical issues are being brought to the world organization. A host of codes of ethics and conduct are being elaborated at the UN. The Charter itself is one of the boldest codes of ethics ever drafted for the behavior of very powerful institutions: armed nations. Although its rules are all too often broken by its members, it nurtures progressively a better behavior, a greater understanding and an improved general moral political atmosphere. Our scientific and industrial age has yielded incredible progress to the human race and we should be immensely grateful for it. But this success perhaps led us to believe that material achievement and intelligence were the apex of civilization. There no longer seemed to be any need for ethics, purity, morality, compassion, love and spirituality. This unnecessary poverty of our age is now being increasingly recognized. Humanity needs also to probe the immense possibilities of its heart and of its soul. This is the great new challenge which has been raised very forcefully by a younger generation tired of war, hatred, hypocrisy and injustices.

I have a Christ in my office. My colleague next door has a statue of Shiva. U Thant had a Buddha in his room. Each of us, be he from North or from South, from East or from West, has his own way of expressing faith in the human race and destiny. When a conflict breaks out any place on the globe, we are all in agreement that it must be stopped, that people cannot be allowed to kill each other, that life must be revered everywhere, that the human person is the supreme care of all our efforts. So, despite its imperfections, the UN is becoming one of the greatest and most beautiful sagas of modern times. King Paul of Greece saw it as a "cathedral where we can worship what is best in each other." Pope John Paul II said that we were the stonecutters and artisans of a cathedral which we might never see in its finished beauty. I would not have dreamed that when I joined the United Nations a third of a century ago. The scope of the UN has widened in every direction, owing to the imperatives of a new global, interdependent world. But people do not really know how vast and vital its activities are. The tapestry of its work encompasses the total condition of humankind on this planet. All this is part of one of the most prodigious pages of evolution. It will require the detachment and objectivity of future historians to appraise fully what happened in the last third of our century and to understand what the real significance of the United Nations was.

Meditation, prayer, dream, hope, vision, faith, guidance, foresight and planning all go hand in hand in so many ways. The tall Secretariat building of the UN is an edifice of human hope and dream jutting into the universe and receiving from that universe increasingly clearer messages. Perhaps the time has come when we will understand the full significance of our cosmic evolution. Year round people from all creeds and cultures gather at the UN to design a better future for the world. And they will succeed. Our children will know a better future, a more peaceful world, an unprecedented fulfillment of individual human life and consciousness.

Little by little, a planetary prayer book is thus being composed by an increasingly united humanity seeking its oneness, its happiness, its consciousness, its peace, its justice and its full participation in the continuous process of creation and miracle of life. Once again, but this time on a universal scale, humankind is seeking no less than its reunion with the "divine," its transcendence into ever higher forms of life. Hindus call our earth Brahma, or God, for they rightly see no difference between our earth and the divine. This ancient simple truth is slowly dawning again upon humanity. Its full flowering will be the real, great new story of humanity, as we are about to enter our cosmic age and to become what we were always meant to be: the planet of God.

7

The Four Cries of Humanity

U Thant was a great man because he was able to distill from the immense complexity of the surrounding world and from his observations of life a vision, a few basic, deeply felt principles. These were always the same: that every human being had physical, mental, moral and spiritual qualities and needs. He established a hierarchy among them, for in his view the final objective of human evolution was spiritual fulfillment. This inspired his entire life and work.

I knew U Thant well and I have read assiduously much of what he has said and written. And everywhere I can find the expression of the influence of this simple but so fundamental classification of human attributes and needs. Therein lie the fourfold cries of humanity or basic stages of evolution: for optimum physical life, mental life, moral life and spiritual life.

The Cry for Physical Life

U Thant was very outspoken when he expressed his belief in the sanctity of life, non-violence and the non-harming of human beings. For example, in a speech on education in 1967, he said:

"I have been trained all my life to regard human life as sacred. I abhor violence and violent death. I do not particularly worry much about my own life, but I do worry a great deal about the children of today. How they should be taught, how they should be brought up, what kind of life they should live and what values they should cherish. I do not particularly distinguish between the lives of my own children and the lives of the children of other people. Nor do I distinguish between Burmese lives and American lives and Russian lives and Chinese lives. It is life itself that is threatened."

U Thant always took an unequivocal stand for the sovereignty of life. He condemned war and violence in all their forms. His speeches abound in beautiful statements on non-violence and on the universal law of love, reverence and respect for all living beings. He was against war, against nuclear weapons and all armaments, against poverty and all human suffering. He never hesitated one moment to express his full commitment to life and non-violence, often to the great annoyance of the powerful, armed and wealthy.

The Cry for Mental Fulfillment

U Thant was a teacher. Although he usually didn't resort to such extreme language, he began the above speech as follows: "I am going to speak with a feeling of trepidation because I am going to speak about something which is very close to my heart: education." What he saw foremost in education was the fulfillment of the human mind. There can be no conscious life if a human being does not receive a proper education. Otherwise, how can he understand and enjoy the beauty of life? He pleaded constantly for the education of the children of the poor and for the work of UNESCO. But for him education was even more: it was a preparation for life as a member of a universal, human family. Therefrom arose his great love and support for the international schools and his proposal for a United Nations University. He believed that only through proper education would we be able to build the world of peace and kindness humanity has always dreamed of. It was one of his staunchest beliefs.

The Cry for Morality

Here U Thant had a long list of cravings: e.g., his wish for truthfulness between nations. He wanted nations to be true to each other, not to lie, not to exaggerate, not to cheat, not to start from those falsehoods called "bargaining positions" which so often mar international diplomacy.

He craved for understanding between nations, non-violence, generosity, live and let live. He believed in the magic of love and compassion in international relations. All this is reflected in his statements on apartheid, racism, colonialism, violations of human rights and whatever else is reprehensible on this planet. He was not just re-

peating the political slogans of the day, he was speaking from a
sound, all-out commitment to human life. U Thant's great strength,
the alpha and omega of all his action and thinking, were the supremacy and centrality of the human person. In his farewell speech
to Planetary Citizens on December 17, 1971, he said:

"What was my basic approach to all problems? What was the 'system' I employed? I would describe it as the human approach or the
central importance of the human element in all problems: political,
economic, social, colonial, racial, etc. And when I say the human approach, some of you are aware of my philosophy, of my basic concept
regarding the human community and the human situation."

And once again he repeated his four categories:

"There are certain variations and priorities in values. In my view, an
ideal man or an ideal woman is endowed with four virtues, four qualities: physical qualities, mental qualities, moral qualities, and above all,
spiritual qualities."

The Cry for Spirituality

The world U Thant saw around him, the system of Western
values culminating in the UN, was far from being the spiritual garden he was dreaming of. The UN was doing much for the physical
and mental well-being of humanity, and it was also fostering the
birth of world morality in many fields. But the world organization
did not possess the all-encompassing spirituality he found so necessary. And yet he firmly believed that spirituality would be the next
stage of evolution, transcending our earlier periods of material and
intellectual progress. He believed that only spirituality and not bal-
ance of power, interests or reason would bring about peace and justice on earth. For him, spirituality was the ultimate harmony, the individual's and society's right perception of the cosmos, of our planet
and of all human relations. This was for him the highest stage of development humanity could reach, the ultimate, fullest realization of
human destiny in the universe. Once you find your right, harmonious place in the total order of things, then love, compassion, understanding, good behavior, reverence for life and peaceful relations
with others automatically ensue. Then you have reached enlightenment and you feel in yourself the plenitude of the miracle of life.
Then you are a peaceful, happy, serene, fulfilled, untroubled, harmonious, well-functioning cosmos which knows its place amid the myr-

iads of cosmoses of the universe. U Thant's view of harmony resembled very much that of Confucius, who saw in government the art of achieving ultimate human harmony on earth and with the universe. It is revealing that the word "government" in Chinese means: to put things in the right place, to achieve harmony.

Unfortunately we are still far from this stage of evolution. The Western world has succeeded tremendously in the physical, intellectual and scientific spheres, but it has not yet perceived the virtues of harmony and the fathomless treasures of moral and spiritual fulfillment. Power, glory and wealth are still the dominant cravings. The heart and soul of Western man have not followed the development of his mind. As U Thant said in his speech to Planetary Citizens:

"I am in no sense anti-intellectual, but the stress of education in the schools of highly developed societies, as I have stated on many previous occasions, is primarily on the development of the intellect or in physical excellence. To me, moral and spiritual aspects of life are far more important than the physical and intellectual aspects of life."

In his kind and unobtrusive way, U Thant was far ahead of our time. He saw for the entire world what he had discovered for himself, namely, that thought, meditation, prayer, contemplation, inner search and interrogation are the links between the miracle of human life and the universe. Good physical lives—respect for one's body; good mental lives—the acquisition of knowledge; good moral lives— the practice of love; and good spiritual lives—the practice of prayer and meditation, merge individual life with divinity, the universe, infinity, and lead to a wondrous respect for all creation and a deep gratitude for the miraculous gift of life in a vast, mysterious universe. This is the royal path to world peace and happiness, not the path of power, wealth and vainglory, which belong to an earlier, more primitive period of evolution.

Humanity is finding its right way, slowly but surely. Much has been achieved for the physical and mental improvement of human lives, but it has not yet reached the entire world since so many of our brethren and sisters are still living in poverty, sickness and ignorance. But in a great part of the world life now is generally long, good and healthy, and a school child knows more than any earlier king or emperor in all of human history. Good bodies and good minds bring us nearer to divinity and to a full consciousness of our place in the universe. The same is true of morality and spirituality: they are fundamental parts of human ascent. But here we have still great progress to achieve. There is much corruption and immorality in today's world. Mammon and not the God of the universe is on the altars of our societies. How small we have become, how unnecessarily our vision has shrunk, how limited our ambitions are amid our material and intellectual achievements!

There is need for a vast moral and spiritual renaissance to set our conquests at their right place within the magnificent order of things in the universe. The people are crying for moral and spiritual values. They are tired of wars, immorality and lack of meaning of the mystery of life. They know that the absence of moral and spiritual order means lack of civilization, that without such order a society is on the brink of decadence.

In our human garden, there are many flowers, many beliefs, many religions, there are even plants without flowers and faiths without God. For many God is the symbol of perfection, of that fullest life, knowledge, love, soul-consciousness and supreme happiness humans have been seeking since the beginnings of time.

U Thant often spoke of the law of *karma*, the principle that every action has a reaction, good or evil. I am grateful to him for having taught me this law. I hope that his message will continue to spread, that the law of a good *karma* will operate throughout the world and that more and more people will understand that the key to the future rests in their own garden, in their potential four and a half billion commitments to peace, love, kindness and human fraternity. To the concept of the noosphere, or sphere of the mind encompassing all humans, we would be well advised to add those of a karmasphere, or sphere of good actions, mettasphere,[1] or sphere of love, animasphere,[2] or sphere of the universal soul. Then humanity could progress and lift itself upwards towards a total communion with God, the universe and eternity.

[1] From the Buddhist concept of *metta*, or love and kindness towards all living beings.
[2] From the Latin *anima*, soul.

PART II

The Global Transcendence
of Human Values

8

An Education Through Love

Humanity has discovered of late a great number of interdependencies which encompass our entire planet. The UN Stockholm Conference on the Environment brought to light the concept of the biosphere: a little sphere only a few miles thick enrobing the globe and containing all life of our solar system. The interdependencies of our environment, of our water, of our seas and oceans, of our air, of our energy and resources have revealed that we are all part of an extremely complex, marvelous fabric of life, of a unique, astonishing living body in the universe, which must be the object of our utmost care. Also, during the last century, humanity has added its own list of teeming man-made interdependencies through science, trade, business, transportation, communications, international exchanges, travel and tourism. Finally, we have discovered our indissoluble interdependence with the past and with the future. Our planet and its precious cargo of life advance in time as a huge, complex, miraculous, evolving intergalactic body.

In this vast list of global interdependencies, there is one which is particularly vital: *our children.* Humanity's children form the most precious network of human interdependence, the link between past and future without which all other interdependencies would cease to be relevant, for without the children humanity would soon cease to be.

When I think of the family, I always remember the beginning of Rousseau's *Contrat social*, in which he says that the only natural society is the family. The family is indeed the most highly interdependent society, perfected over millions of years of evolution. In it, grandparents, father, mother and children normally adapt to each other in many mysterious and marvelous ways, among which the most important one, insufficiently studied by humankind, is love. The first education that the little baby receives is entirely through love, particularly the mother's love. This great unexplored concept has been vastly underestimated as a means of increasing the knowledge, peace, understanding and interdependence of humanity and the general functioning of our planet. It is rarely used as an instrument of international relations. Political personalities, experts, scientists and diplomats, in our age of dry reason, rarely use the word "love," neglecting its cardinal value to achieve a more harmonious, well-functioning, happy human society and planetary habitat. And yet, to conduct our mysterious and miraculous journey in the universe we need above all faith, hope and love. And of the three, as so many saints and prophets have proclaimed, the most effective is love.

The greatest group of people to which we must henceforth direct our attention is the *human family*. Again, the Buddha, Christ and all great visionaries, philosophers and prophets saw the fundamental unity of humankind even though they lived in small separated societies scattered over the globe. Today, it is a completely different story. Today our world society of more than four billion people knows very well what is happening across the waters on the other side of the world. It is the transformation of this last-born and greatest society of all *into a family* which is the fundamental task of our time. How can we bring about this larger community? How can we find the natural, optimum, harmonious adaptation, relations and understanding between nations, races, religions, languages, institutions, enterprises, ideologies and professions? The search for a peaceful, reciprocal enrichment of all these diverse groups within one perfect human family is our next fundamental task on our evolutionary path. So far in history, humanity itself has been the great neglected orphan.

Our future family will be that of our children. If we give the right education to the fifteen thousand children born every hour and make them feel part of the beautiful human family and its mysterious physical, mental, moral and spiritual interdependencies, then we will obtain a better world. We must give a global education to all the world's children, teach them about the miracle and sanctity of life, the necessity of love for our planet, for our great human family, for the heavens and for the Creator of all these marvels. We must teach them rules of good behavior towards our global home and all our human sisters and brothers, so as to ensure peace, justice and happiness for all, and make our planet a showcase in the universe, as God wants it to be. This is the true, ultimate purpose of our evolution and of our efforts.

If we can teach right from the primary school the type of interdependent society into which children are born, then we will progress towards a truly good human family on a unique and well-run planet. Our minds must be directed towards these newcomers, towards the new human society being formed hour after hour under our very eyes by the arrival of new children. Through the education of all the children of the world and the right education about their world, we will prepare the novel planetary society which is in the making and which begins to be visible in the United Nations.

Recent history has shown that the old ways of taking the world by force, conquering and dividing, fragmenting, hating, fearing, arming, subverting, ruling and destroying no longer work in the interdependent circumstances of our planet. We must now try other ways which should be thoroughly studied by the best minds and applied by the political leaders of our planet: the ways of love, understanding, cooperation, altruism, justice and harmony, the superiority of which has been proved so irrefutably by the oldest, most advanced and most natural of all societies, *the family*.

9

Of Science and Love

One day at the UN I received in the mail a big volume written by a religious scholar on the history of the philosophy of science. The book was accompanied by a letter in which the author expressed the wish to see me after I had read his book.

I began to read it and I was deeply enthralled by it. The UN was about to hold a major conference on science and technology, and such a work on the deeper, philosophical meanings of science and technology was very timely.

Alas, in an active position like mine there is very little time to read more than a dozen printed pages a day. But I set my mind on it, determined to gain valuable knowledge. Unfortunately, the book was so hard to read, so dense with philosophy and theories, that each time I resumed my reading I had to start from the beginning. I knew it was hopeless and that I would never be able to finish it. I looked in vain for a conclusion or summary in which the author would have listed his main findings. But there was none. It was a book meant to be read from beginning to end. There was no escape from it.

So I put it aside, together with piles of other books sent to me by authors, awaiting the hypothetical time when I would have sufficient leisure to catch up with my reading.

A couple of weeks later the author called me and asked for an appointment. In the meantime a diplomat had told me that he was a very fine scholar, perhaps a little too much in love with matters of the mind and not enough in touch with reality. He asked me to guide him towards the practical problems encountered in the UN.

So the author showed up in my office one day. He was a middle-aged, tall, distinguished, well-bred, extremely good-looking gentleman. I greeted him, congratulated him on his fine book, seized the volume from a shelf and said:

"Alas, as much as I regret it, I have not been able to read your work, except for a few dozen pages. It is a scholarly book, very hard to read for a busy person like me. I have tried my best, but every time I had to start all over again. Finally I gave it up and I am afraid I will never finish it. I am sorry, but this happens frequently to people in my position."

I asked him if he didn't have a summary or conclusions of his book.

He dryly answered no.

I asked him if he could not prepare one:

"Your work and conclusions could be of immense value to the UN, especially to my colleagues in charge of the Conference on Science and Technology. I often regret that we do not have any philosophers at the UN. You have spent a lifetime on this momentous subject. Couldn't you summarize your findings for the Secretary-General and other concerned officials? I could advise you to send them copies of your book, but I know all too well that they do not have the time either. Secretary-General Waldheim has warned us all in this house: he will not read any text that is more than a page long. It is hard for us to comply, for it is much more difficult to write one page than twenty."

But he remained adamant and said wryly:

"My book cannot be summarized. It is the story of humanity's efforts in science and technology. It must be read from beginning to end."

"Couldn't you give us at least your conclusions, the philosophical considerations you think the delegates to the UN Conference on Science and Technology should have high on their minds?"

He remained silent.

To break the ice and pursue the conversation, I asked him abruptly:

"Do you treat the subject of love in your book?"

His superb impassivity left him all at once. He looked utterly astonished, examined me from top to bottom, then looked around my office as if wondering what kind of a crazy man the UN had in its service. I was glad that a large Crucifix was hanging behind my desk, protecting me from his total contempt.

He finally uttered these words, which fell condescendingly from his lips, as if he wanted to distance himself entirely from the nonsense I had said:

"Love! Love! What on earth has love to do with science?"

The moment had come to stick a banderilla into his intellectualism. I answered:

"Yes. Perfectly. I mean love. It has always struck me that love is one of the mightiest and most effective scientific concepts there is in this world. In my case, it is primarily through love that I see my relationships with the total earth, its people, my colleagues, my work, the universe, infinity and God. But to give you a more immediate and down-to-earth example: when a young man and a girl fall in love with each other, what happens at that moment? Isn't it a prodigious synthetic, unitary answer to a multitude of scientific questions? Two extremely complicated cosmoses made up of trillions of cells and immemorial genetic experiences decide to unite and to continue the chain of life! What a prodigious and momentous decision! Science could never give a satisfactory answer to such a colossal biological problem. And yet love does it in the most mysterious, simple, effective, pleasurable and miraculous way. Hence love is in your domain as it is in mine. I would even go so far as to say that love for life, passion for life, fascination with life is the prime motive of true scientific investigation. Human love for knowing and piercing the amazing creation is part of the spiritual process."

He had listened very carefully to me and when I finished his entire behavior changed forthwith. His face lit up, became warm and more human, he got up on his feet, paced my office up and down, thinking, smiling and rubbing his hands. Suddenly he stopped abruptly in front of me and asked:

"Do you have a Bible?"

"Yes."

"Could you give it to me?"

I handed him a venerable leather-bound volume whose pages he turned rapidly. He finally found the passage he had been looking for and pointed at a text which he asked me to read. It was from the Proverbs and it said:

"There are three things, nay, four, which are too wonderful for me to understand: the way of an eagle in the air; the way of a serpent on a rock; the way of a ship on the seas; and the way of a man with a maiden."

He then relaxed into a warm, friendly attitude and said to me in a humble way:

"You have taught me a lesson and reminded me of a very basic truth. I will not forget it."

The time had now come to fulfill my promise to my friend the diplomat:

"You see, the UN Conference on Science and Technology is also in the end a question of love. Reason and interest alone will not do it. Only love for our brethren and sisters in the poorer parts of the world, and love for our entire beautiful planet, will allow us to find the answers to that great conference."

And I was able then to give him the pertinent information on that lastest UN venture in which at first he had shown little interest.

Ever since then we have been great friends. He took an active part in the conference and wrote several excellent short, action-oriented, down-to-earth papers.

And each time when I receive some of his writings, I look up at my Crucifix and I see a little, delighted smile of complicity on the loving lips of Jesus.

* * *

I have one further story on that subject:

One day Professor M. from the Institute of Life in Paris visited me to see if his organization could be of help to the United Nations in some of the matters of current concern, in particular the International Year of the Child, the UN Conference on Science and Technology and the World Assembly on Aging. We discussed several possibilities, for I had high regard for this association of some of the world's greatest scientists dealing with human life. I always derive much knowledge and advance perceptions of new global problems from their congresses and communications.

At one stage of our conversation I asked him point-blank:

"Why don't you deal with the subject of love in your institution?"

Like the religious scholar, he could not hide his disbelief at what I had said.

He mumbled grudgingly: "Love, love? What has love to do with the science of life?"

I commented:

"Isn't the love of a mother for her child a great mysterious reality which should be the subject of scientific investigation? Isn't humanity's love for its children the alpha and omega of the International Year of the Child? Isn't love for our older people the key to the World Assembly on Aging? Shouldn't your institute study and foster the concept of love for the improvement of the human condition on our planet?"

He thought for a moment and came up with an answer:

"We are dealing with it, but in a different, more scientific way. It has been proven recently that the physical and mental development of a child depends in a very large degree on his affective environment, especially the mother and the family. This has become a major subject of research among pediatricians and specialists of children."

I looked at my Crucifix and wondered once more in my life why scientists had always to resort to a special jargon, instead of using the beautiful words inherited from millennia of evolution. Love is scoffed at as being non-scientific. Then the word "environment" becomes fashionable and love reappears under the term "affective environment"! What a complicated, devious world! What a lack of courage to be simple, straightforward and to speak from the heart understandably to all peoples. What is wrong, I ask you, with the word "love"?

After he left my office I made a number of telephone calls to my colleagues and said to them:

"Henceforth I would advise you to use generously the words 'affective environment': for the child, for youth, for the handicapped, for older people, for relations between nations, for our planet and for the entire human family. Love doesn't sell as yet, but quality of life and affective environment are now respectable scientific notions. Let us therefore use them up to the brim."

But in the evening when I came home and looked at my wife and children, I thought that affective environment was a very poor substitute for what I felt for them. O humanity! When will you decide to restore the great, simple, noble, tested, down-to-earth common-sense values which from time immemorial have been the foundations of our civilization and happiness? Why do the scientists dislike so much the words "love, beauty, faith, joy, happiness, kindness, goodness, fascination, ecstasy, God," etc.? Why? Why don't we all revolt against the heartless scientific jargon and state our right to an understandable, inspired, heartfelt language?

10

The Issue of Human Rights

I have learned during my many years at the United Nations that the nobler an objective the more difficult it is to achieve. The four most difficult issues in world affairs still remain disarmament—i.e., a planet devoid of arms, especially nuclear arms—the development of the poor countries, human rights, and world democracy, or the participation of people in designing their own fate and future on this planet. Of the four, perhaps human rights has fared best. Where do we stand on this crucial issue today?

There are two basic aspects to human rights. On the one hand, there is the formulation of what the rights of the human being should be, and secondly, there is the implementation of the philosophy. As regards the concepts of human rights, undoubtedly since the adoption of the Charter of the United Nations immense progress has been achieved. Truly, I would never have expected, coming out of the Second World War, that humanity would be able to draft a philosophy of life through intergovernmental committees. We have today, after these several years, a Universal Declaration of Human Rights complemented by detailed Covenants on political and civil rights, economic, cultural and social rights. If you take these texts together you have a beautiful, unique charter of what human life should be for each individual on this planet. I cannot emphasize enough that this is one of the great achievements of the human race in recent years: it has been able to define a collective philosophy of what human rights should be. There is often great beauty in these texts. I wish that the Universal Declaration of Human Rights would be taught in every school on earth. Beyond this universal text, over the last decades, a systematic effort has been made to look at human rights from every possible aspect. There are not only the rights of the human person as such, but humans have also a race, a sex, physical and mental capacities or incapacities, and an age. Over the years, the Universal Declaration and the Covenants have been complemented by a series of special declarations for these various groups. There is little doubt that regarding racial equality the world has changed profoundly since 1945. Despite a few last pockets of resistance, immense progress has been accomplished in world-wide recognition of the equality of races. There is further the example of the Declaration of the Rights of the Child the twentieth anniversary of which was celebrated during the International Year of the Child. Much misery still affects the children of this world: ten per cent of the newly born die before one year is over and another four per cent die before five years have passed; several hundred million children go hungry; one hundred eighty million children still do not go to school; fifteen million children under the age of fifteen are working despite the provisions of that Declaration.

The world has also looked at the rights of women. This is one of the earliest works of the United Nations. It culminated in a World Women's Conference, held in Mexico in 1975, and another conference in 1980 in Denmark to see what progress has been achieved world-wide in implementing the equality of the sexes.

Another problem has strongly come to the fore. It concerns the physical and mental characteristics of people. We have, unfortunately, four hundred fifty million handicapped persons on this planet. They need special protection. That protection has been laid down in the Declaration of the Rights of the Mentally Retarded of 1971, in the Declaration of the Rights of the Handicapped of 1975, and in the Declaration of the Rights of the Blind of 1980.

We see therefore the Universal Declaration of Human Rights being refined and complemented year after year. The United Nations first World Assembly on Aging is expected to consider a declaration of the rights of the hundreds of millions of elderly persons on our planet.

These conceptual frameworks of human rights will probably never be complete because our concept of life is changing with time. New unprecedented preoccupations do appear and make claims for new types of human rights. For example, of late there has been a great preoccupation with the rights of the individual to be protected from incursions in his private life—for example computerization, and scientific, genetic and technological tampering with life. The whole question of human rights, from the development of the child in the womb of the mother to the moment of death, has been examined by the World Health Organization. In the not too distant future another problem will come up in the United Nations, namely, the right to a certain quality of life. A good environment is beginning to be perceived as a basic human right. As the years pass we will also hear of a Declaration of the Right Not to Kill and Not to Be Killed, not even in the name of a nation. It is very interesting that the provisions on human rights of the UN Charter speak of the realization of human rights and fundamental freedoms for all without distinction as to race, sex, language or religion. But the word "nation" has been carefully omitted. Today, you can still "rightfully" be asked to kill another human being in the name of a nation. Conscientious objectors have brought this problem to the United Nations and the time will come when a human being will be given the right not to kill and not to be killed.

Someday there will also be the right to live on a planet devoid of armaments, in particular nuclear armaments. This should be a basic right of each human being. Life on this planet requires a certain number of fundamental obligations of states. One of these is not to endanger life and the planet with cataclysmic anti-human armaments. The whole concept of human rights must evolve with the problem of nationhood. You are well protected as a member of a state or nation but not as a member of the human race. From the moment you become a refugee, you no longer have any rights left. There are today on this planet more than twelve million refugees, half of them children. They have very few legal rights. They are living in camps set up by the United Nations. Eventually they will be given new rights, but it takes such a long time to find a country of "asylum." Human rights are recommended internationally but they are granted by national jurisdictions. This is not just. The human person and planetary citizenship must be given absolute priority over national citizenship. It cannot be otherwise.

The second aspect of human rights concerns implementation. We now possess very beautiful texts and norms. We have a body of world directives—not legislation—which command admiration and respect. But the question of implementation is quite another story.

Implementation of human rights can take place at the national level, at the regional level and at the world level.

At the national level it is the duty of states which have adhered to the Conventions to implement their provisions. National legislation can full well protect human rights and one could envisage a world in which each nation would protect them adequately. But here we run into difficulties. Many nations do not believe that they are in the service of human beings. They claim that citizens owe allegiance to the state, a religion, a way of life or a philosophical concept. There are on this planet a number of states which require highest allegiance to a religion. In some of them the constitution is a religious text. These states may require that you be of a certain religion to be a citizen! It is quite a problem, for example, to see how human rights of women are implemented in countries which function under ancient religious codes. In these countries the law of a religious book is the supreme law, not the recommendations of the United Nations. In other nations the state or an ideology has supreme priority. As a result the individual has to submit to the priority requirements of the state or ideology, with the possible loss of personal rights. In other countries primacy is given to a philosophical concept, for example, the philosophy and practice of liberty: freedom of expression, freedom of activity, freedom to accumulate wealth. But this too can lead to much excess, monopoly and injustice. In the poorer countries, the most important preoccupations are survival, food, health, education, employment and dignity. We still live in a very imperfect, checkered world, a world of dazzling inequality and diversity of conditions, endowments, aspirations and dreams. Nevertheless, the world community is asking states to accept at least those common denominators of the rights of the human being which have been agreed to in the United Nations. Even that implementation is far from being satisfactory.

There are only two continents where human rights are protected by regional conventions and institutions. Western Europe has had a European Convention of Human Rights for more than twenty-five years. It has a Court of Human Rights. An individual, a non-governmental organization, or a state can introduce a complaint of violations of human rights to that court. When the court has taken a decision the state has to implement it, either by paying indemnities or redressing the injustice. This is the only place on the planet where an individual has effective recourse against national mistreatment in a court with international jurisdiction. Recently, progress has been made in Latin America: the first Latin American Court of Human Rights has been established in Costa Rica, but only a state and not an individual can have recourse to it. How far we are from the day when individuals will be able to seek redress against violations of human rights by states to a world human rights court!

How does the situation look on a world-wide basis? Well, here the situation is not good at all. True enough, we have Covenants. But the first question is: who has ratified those conventions? Out of one hundred and fifty-seven member states of the United Nations not more than a third have ratified them. In other words, many countries of the world do not even consider themselves bound by these texts. And there are some very large countries among them!

When you look more closely at the Covenants, you will find many escape clauses. Some of them contain a protocol which provides that a government accepts that individual petitions may be addressed to the United Nations. But the number of countries which have accepted that protocol is limited to about two dozen. There are thus less than two out of ten countries on this planet that allow an individual or a non-governmental organization to turn to the international community with a complaint under the Covenants! Of course, an individual can send any complaint to the UN. These complaints are handled under procedures which still reflect the reluctance of nations to be internationally probed, criticized and condemned. The first official complaint ever dealt with under the Covenants was a complaint from private citizens of a Latin American country. The government of that country was condemned, but it does not have to abide by the decision or redress the situation if it does not want to. There is no forceful implementation!

This shows the enormous distance still to be covered both conceptually and practically until there is a satisfactory implementation of human rights on this planet. Is it a desperate situation? Not necessarily. It has taken humanity hundreds of years to get rid of slavery and it has done so. Human ascent requires that we work at such issues relentlessly. We have at least a Universal Declaration of Human Rights. It was adopted at a time when there were only fifty-one nations in the world organization. Today the United Nations is as universal as its Declaration. For the first time in the entire evolution of humankind the dream of all the great prophets and visionaries has been fulfilled: now on this planet we have a universal organization. This will progressively force governments to abide by the new ethical concepts which are being forged in humanity's collective institutions. The chances for progress are immensely fostered by the mere existence of this universal organization. This is why I appeal to all men and women of this planet to give their fullest support to their universal organization, because the better, the stronger and more respected it is, the greater our chances will be to see our individual human rights finally implemented by the states to which we "belong." It is not only in the interest of nations to have the United Nations. It is of even far greater interest for individuals to have the United Nations, so that we will finally obtain from our states, governments, institutions, legislators and executives respectful behavior towards the individual. A state and an institution have no life. Only people are endowed with the miracle of life. They should have priority over states and institutions. Without people states and institutions would be empty shells. They should never forget it. Laws, governments, institutions, religions, associations, corporations and the United Nations have been created by "we, the people," for the improvement of the life of human beings, for the physical, mental, moral and spiritual fulfillment of the individual. The story of humanity is the story of the flowering of life of individuals who alone can live, love, be happy and procreate.

We must thank God and those who have perished in the Second World War that the Charter has not forgotten this and that it has included the issue of human rights as one of its most fundamental preoccupations. But we must help accelerate the process, which is far too slow, for after the rights of the human person have been taken care of there remain other rights to consider, in particular the rights of the planet itself and the rights of future generations.[1]

I have worked in this organization for an entire adult's lifetime. I saw in the Second World War two very civilized countries, Germany and France, lash out at each other like savages. I was born on their common border. I could see the other country across the river from my window. I was told during my youth that France was the greatest country on earth and then the Germans came and told us that they were the greatest. Both sides gave us guns to shoot at peo-

---

[1] A Draft Charter for Nature has been submitted by the government of Zaire to the General Assembly. The Jacques Cousteau Society for its part has prepared a Draft Declaration of Rights of Future Generations which it wants to see adopted by the United Nations.

ple who were human brethren, who had the same names—who spoke the same language; who had the same faces; and who were our blood relatives. Nevertheless, in the name of a nation, we were clothed in different "uniforms" and asked to kill each other. This is no longer tolerable at the present stage of evolution. This planet was not created for international mass murders. It was not born cut up in borders, nations and groups. It is and has always been an interdependent planet, a complete biosphere, a sphere of life in which all human beings are sacred irrespective of their group affiliations. It might be some time before the political world catches up with this reality. But I have seen enough progress during my lifetime to believe in the success of the human race on our miraculous little planet in the universe. We should all remember these good words by Edmund Burke:

All that is necessary for evil to flourish is that good people do nothing.

11

The Right Not to Kill

In every epoch of history there are a few exceptional human beings who are blessed with a correct vision of the place of the human person on earth and in the universe. This vision is always basically the same:

— it recognizes the oneness and supremacy of the human family, irrespective of color, sex, creed, nation or any other distinctive characteristics;

— it recognizes each individual human being as a unique miracle of divine origin, a cosmos of his own, never to be repeated again in all eternity;

— it rejects all violence as being contrary to the sanctity and uniqueness of life, and advocates love, tolerance, truth, cooperation and reverence for life as the only civilized means of achieving a peaceful and happy society;

— it preaches love and care for our beautiful and so diverse planet in the fathomless universe;

— it sees each human life and society as part of an eternal stream of time and ever ascending evolution;

— it recognizes that the ultimate mysteries of life, time and the universe will forever escape the human mind and therefore bends in awe and humility before these mysteries and God;

— it advocates gratitude and joy for the privilege of being admitted to the banquet of life;

— it preaches hope, faith, optimism and a deep commitment to the moral and ethical virtues of peace and justice distilled over eons of time as the foundations for further human ascent.

Only people with this simple vision, unmarred by political and personal interests, do ultimately survive in the memory of humankind. They are the great religious leaders, saints, philosophers, artists and humanists of all times. They sing a breath-taking hymn to life, to our planet and to the universe. They deal with the fundamental truths.

Our time has been fortunate to count several such great people, whose number might well be on the increase. We were blessed with a Gandhi, an Albert Schweitzer, a Sri Aurobindo, an H. G. Wells, a Teilhard de Chardin, a Toynbee and, nearer to us, Dag Hammarskjöld, U Thant, Pablo Casals and Mother Teresa. Last but not least, it was the turn of the American soil to produce such a great human being, Martin Luther King. It did it in the true American way: Martin Luther King had his roots in Africa, bore the name of a European and professed a Christian faith born in the Middle East. His life and work overflowed with the unmistakable accents of true vision. One could quote endless thoughts and words of his which make one's heart vibrate, which inspire, which elevate, which make us feel better, greater and proud to be human. Everything he did and said bore the stamp of that same great human dream which is also being sought under the cupola of the UN. This is why he was described as a first citizen of the world, a man of all ages and of all continents. We find in him the same ultimate message left to us by Dag Hammarskjöld and U Thant, namely, that love is the secret of secrets, the great transcending force which alone can break the nemesis of war and violence. These were his words in this regard.

To the crowd gathered outside his bombed home in Montgomery: "We must love our white brothers no matter what they do to us. We must make them know that we love them." In an address to a huge gathering in Washington in 1957: "We must never be bitter—if we indulge in hate, the new order will only be the old order. We must meet hate with love, physical force with soul force." After being jailed in Montgomery: "Blood may flow in the streets of Montgomery before we receive our freedom, but it must be our blood that flows and not that of the white man. We must not harm a single hair on the head of our white brothers." In the sermon "Loving Your Enemies": "To our most bitter opponents we say: Do to us what you will, and we shall continue to love you. Throw us in jail, and we shall still love you. Bomb our homes and threaten our children, and we shall still love you."

Martin Luther King and Pablo Casals were foremost in reminding us of a fundamental human right which is not often heard of in UN debates: the right not to kill and not to be killed, not even in the name of a nation.

Many facets of human rights have indeed been studied, defined and codified over the years, but that one has remained surrounded by a strange silence!

During our human evolution and especially during the last few decades it has become increasingly clear that each individual human life is an astounding miracle. Scientists stand in wonder before their genetic discoveries and the functioning of the human being. The more they discover, the more each human appears as an incredible cosmos which has never existed before and will never exist again in the same form in all eternity. All great visionaries, religious leaders, prophets, philosophers and ethical luminaries knew that by intuition thousands of years ago. Great artists, poets and writers have proclaimed it throughout the course of human history. Pablo Casals and Martin Luther King were two of the latest to proclaim it in the most moving terms and in visible action. Now science is confirming it in its own astonishing ways. There is no doubt that, of all life forms on our planet, humanity is the only one that can elevate itself above its condition, uncover a reality which was closed to its senses, comprehend outer space, inner space and ever larger and smaller infinites, conceive God and transcend itself continuously above its earthly abode. This is why, the more we advance, the more we stand in awe before this miraculous, mysterious, incomprehensible, mind-boggling cosmos called a human person.

What conclusion must we draw from this? Pablo Casals had the artist's straight answer when he said: "If I am a miracle that God or nature has made, how could I kill? No, I can't. Or another human being who is a miracle like me, can he kill someone?" He was thus restating a fundamental truth which has been advocated by all great religions and moral codes: "Thou shalt not kill." This law of civilized society is as true today as it was throughout our past history. To break it in any way is to break the fundamental law of civilization. Therefore, at a moment when the entire question of human rights is being so forcefully debated, we must have the courage to place the right of each human person not to kill and not to be killed at the top of the list. This should be the most sacred law of humanity. As one of the most urgent topics for world ecumenism, I would suggest a meeting of the world's religions to agree and proclaim that no human being shall be required to kill in the name of a nation, a religion or any other group.

The time has come to start a new history in this respect. We must establish reverence for life as the cornerstone of civilization: reverence for life not only by individuals, but also by institutions, foremost among them nations. Institutions were created originally for the good and survival of the people. This is their main justification and merit. They have no right to kill or to develop and stockpile incredible arsenals of weapons meant to kill millions of people, possibly all humanity. And the same nations come to the UN and dare to speak about human rights! Do these include the right to life and the right not to kill? Perhaps if we approach the question of disarmament from the fundamental principle of reverence for life, we might achieve better progress. As a humanist and as a member of the human race who has seen so many killings and violations of human rights during his lifetime, I just cannot conceive and accept the idea of a peaceful and orderly planet of armed nations. As we approach the new global age of humanity, we must unequivocally proclaim and enforce this fundamental, sacred and inalienable right and obligation of all human beings on our planet:

THOU SHALT NOT KILL, NOT EVEN IN THE NAME OF A NATION.

12

The Need for World Gratitude

When the bells, muezzins and gongs will ring again

Invited to inaugurate the World Gratitude Center at Thanksgiving Square in Dallas, I reflected deeply and found that, although throughout my life I had been grateful for the gift of life, I had never thought much about the concept itself. I therefore turned to any encyclopedias I could find, including children's encyclopedias, but except for a few words on the celebration of Thanksgiving, I could not find anything.

I was puzzled. I consulted other books and found that the word "gratitude" was well covered only in two: the Bible and my old Latin dictionary. I was not surprised to find it in the Bible, for daily prayer and thanksgiving to God are two main pillars of religion. But the several pages of quotations from Latin authors were a revelation. The Romans had established gratitude—*gratia*—as a profound philosophical concept at the root of their empire and Pax Romana. Gratitude to the gods was a central rule of public Roman life. Then I consulted an old German etymological dictionary inherited from my grandfather, and I found that the words "*Dank*," "thanks," "*tak*" (Danish), "*dank*" (Dutch), etc., came from *denken*, "to think," and meant to remember something agreeable that had happened or had been given to you. At the UN I consulted colleagues from different lands, and I got some fascinating answers: the Greek *eukharistia* means "expressing joy" (*kharis*); the Arabic *shukran* is related to "sweetness" (sugar); Chinese *shie-shie* meant originally "to decline," for it was a Chinese custom to decline three times before accepting a gift or favor. The different cultural perceptions of "gratitude" were so interesting that the UN Linguistics Club decided to collect its etymology and meanings in as many languages as possible.

The concept seems to be deeply entrenched in all cultures, and it is regretful that in our modern world we have almost forsaken it. We must re-establish gratitude at the center of our global civilization. In tomorrow's planetary society, as in yesterday's Roman Empire, it must be a common spirit occupying the hearts of all citizens. We must conceive of a time when all the billions of humans of this planet, upon rising in the morning, will give thanks to God for the gift of life on our beautiful planet. The bells, the muezzins and the gongs must ring again all over the globe and reverberate into the universe our gratitude, our eucharist or expression of joy for the resurrection of life and of another day. We will never grasp the infinity and eternity of God's creation, but we must at least be joyful for seeing and knowing such a vast and marvelous part of it.

When I think of gratitude, the image of Pablo Casals comes again to my mind. I have seldom met anyone who was able so constantly and so deeply to express his thankfulness for life. When he spoke on that subject, he often ended up in tears, lamenting the incapacity of so many people to understand what an incredible miracle life is.

Another master of mine who shared this view unreservedly was U Thant. His religion was quite fundamental to him and in his memoirs he explained which precepts of Buddhism were particularly useful to him as Secretary-General of the United Nations.[1] One of them was the principle of *metta*, or impersonal love or good will which embraces all beings impartially and spontaneously, friends and foes alike. He considered that each human being was a unique manifestation of the miracle of life in the universe and that consequently we should approach all our human brethren and sisters with deep respect, kindness and wonder. He held that one should never harm or diminish another person, not even verbally. Respect, understanding and love were for him the only correct attitudes towards the prodigy of life. He applied this philosophy very strictly, never criticizing or diminishing other people, never doing harm but, on the contrary, rejoicing at the qualities, achievements, prosperity and good fortune of others. When he disapproved of another person, the worst he would do would be to remain silent.

Turning to the thinkers who had an important influence on him,

[1] *View from the U.N.* (New York: Doubleday & Co., Inc., 1978), Chapter Two, "How I Conceived My Role."

he mentioned Albert Schweitzer and Teilhard de Chardin. Of Albert Schweitzer, he wrote:

> In his *Philosophy of Civilization,* Schweitzer first presented the ethic of "reverence for life"—a theme consistently featured in his life and thought, and the central core of most of his speeches and conversations. . . . He stubbornly pressed hard to bring home his point and developed the theme to encompass wider horizons. Man, he said, must not limit life to the affirmation of man alone; man's ethics must not end with man, but should extend to the universe. He must regain the consciousness of the great chain of life from which he cannot be separated. He preached the necessity of "the will to live an ethical life," which should be the primary motivation of man, and he said life should be for a higher value and purpose—not spent in merely selfish or thoughtless actions. What then results for man is not only a deepening of relationships, but a widening of relationships.

U Thant himself left us some very important teachings, in particular his distinction and hierarchy of the four natures and needs of the human person. If we think for a moment of the human body, its incredible complexity, the marvelous functioning of its trillions of cells, miles of vessels, hundreds of automatisms, a miracle such as the human eye and nervous system, we can but stand in awe before this prodigy. The same is true of the brain, a phenomenal natural, organic computer. And what should we say of the heart, capable of love for our children, family, friends, profession and the entire planet, and last but not least, of the soul, hungry to seek the outer limits of the universe and of time, from creation to the apocalypse? When you think that we have been given such attributes, then there can be only one conclusion, namely, that life is indeed a miracle and that to be a human is an incredible privilege in the universe. We must therefore be grateful for it from morning to evening. In the morning when we rise we should look at the sun, as so many of our brothers and sisters still do in countries like India, in the monasteries and in the rural areas of the world. To pray to the rising sun is to perceive the greatness of the universe and of God, and to recognize the resurrection of the day and of ourselves. In the evening, we must pray again and be thankful for all we have received, learned and enjoyed. As Dag Hammarskjöld put it so beautifully:

> *To everything that has been—Thanks.*
> *For everything that will be—Yes.*

There is so much to be grateful for. It is our duty to give thanks at all times for our admittance to the festival of life, especially in those countries where hunger and poverty have been eliminated. In ancient times it was said that God punished the ungrateful. This is no less true today. For the rich to complain is really to tempt God. Nothing is more shocking indeed than the murmurs and dissatisfaction of the healthy and wealthy. Think of the 500 million hungry in this world, of the 600 million jobless, of the 450 million handicapped, and you will realize, you the healthy and rich, how thankful you should be. The least we must expect from the rich is for them to put an end to their lamentations, waste, greed and unhappiness and to come to the help of their less fortunate brethren and sisters at home and abroad. The first great step towards a happier world is for the well-to-do to acknowledge that life has been good to them and to be grateful to God. If not, what is the use of working so hard to bring about a more prosperous world? Humanity would be well advised to take inspiration from our American Indian brothers, the Senecas, for whom every moment of life is gratitude to the Great Spirit and who express it so beautifully in their greetings, their traditions and in their story of creation.[2]

And we must be grateful to all our Promethean artists—musicians like Bach, Mozart and Beethoven, painters and sculptors like Leonardo and Michelangelo, authors like Shakespeare, Dante and Goethe—for having sung the splendor of life and of the universe and making us vibrate in unison with the beautiful, divine, inscrutable forces of the cosmos.

Thanksgiving Square

Thanksgiving Square is a beautiful place situated in the heart of Dallas, amid gigantic skyscrapers. It is dwarfed by the masses of steel, concrete, glass and aluminum that jut into the air all around it. Nevertheless it manages to prove that smallness with a soul can be as great as if not greater than gianthood without one. While the skyscrapers monotonously look alike, the square abounds with individual features, nature, forms and symbols. A chance has been given here to practically every gradient, shape and geometric form conceiv-

[2] See Elizabeth Tooker, ed., *Native North American Spirituality of the Eastern Woodlands* (Classics of Western Spirituality) (Ramsey, N.J.: Paulist Press, 1979).

able. The most interesting and impressive symbol is the chapel built in the form of a spiral. Those who conceived Thanksgiving Square considered many ideas including that of a Tree of Life. The concept finally retained was suggested by a monk, Brother David Steindl-Rast. He proposed the idea of the spiral, a mysterious, thought-provoking symbol of infinity. As you stand inside, outside or under the chapel, you are taken by its spirit. In your mind you continue to draw the spiral and you visualize it expanding endlessly into the infinite, encompassing the entire universe! Such is the nature of a simple spiral. In the Orient, particularly in India, it was given in cosmic significance long before Western mathematicians became intrigued by it. In Dallas it is a symbol of East-West brotherhood on the American soil.

There is another notable symbol: the stained windows of the chapel come from Chartres, where they were made by the descendants of the craftsmen who fashioned the marvelous glass panes of the glorious French cathedral. Another feature is particularly dear to me, for it is a dream of mine that has come true. During my many years in the United States, I have often missed the sound of European church bells. Since childhood I have loved the soul-stirring, crystalline voice of morning bells which seemed to come from heaven at that very special moment when the day is born again. Bells too represent vibrations which from the tiniest human community on earth reach into the infinite, as a spiral does for the eye and the mind. Bells call the people to prayer and gratitude for daily life as it is so beautifully represented in the famous French painting *The Angelus* by Millet. Today three magnificent bells cast in Annecy, France, adorn Thanksgiving Square and try to stir the souls of the people.

There is only one rectangular shape in the square: the altar on which stands a beautiful, massive glass candelabrum from Ireland. The Hall of Thanksgiving under the chapel offers the sight of immaculate white columns representing various civic associations. Behind these columns flows a sky-blue illuminated water. In the center of the hall, right under the nexus of the spiral, stands a permanent exhibit with a plaque from the UN Meditation Group. Thus the United Nations is present in the temple calling for the prayers of the visitors for the world's first universal peace organization.

It is most interesting to observe the visitors. There are many people from Dallas, especially young people who work in the skyscrapers and who come to dream, relax or have their luncheon in the square, sitting on benches or stone walls, under a tree or near a waterfall. Each person interprets the place in his own way, according to his soul, feelings and inclinations. When I said good-by to the chapel a hippy was sitting there immersed in deep meditation, a prayerbook resting on his lap. I asked the attendant who had been the last person registered in her visitor's book. She said:

"It was a little boy who had come a few days ago to pray to God for rain for the farmers. He came back today to thank God for having made it rain yesterday!" And she added that she could tell scores of similar moving stories.

Thanksgiving Square is a place where you can feel the need of the human being to be grateful for the gift of life, that unique, mysterious outcropping from darkness in the void, that flowering of being under sunlight and the stars. Yes, out of a cell, of a seed, as from the center of a spiral or the impact of a sound, we are grown into a cosmos, a universe of our own, sentient, seeing, feeling, thinking, linked with the great chain of being, from the nucleus of the cell to the vast intergalactic universe, capable of loving and encompassing the entire world in our heart, of feeling the divine, and of lifting ourselves to the Godhead on our own will. You can sense this in the square. It is something unique, and I am grateful that the United Nations has been associated with it. I hope that the spirit of thanksgiving for life will someday encompass the entire planet and illumine peace in the hearts of all human beings.

A Prayer to God at Thanksgiving Square

Dear God, I believe that there is an account on which we have failed You utterly—where we have been regressing rather than progressing of late. We have been able to expand tremendously our physical capacities and to transform profoundly this planet. We have been able to widen immensely the reaches of our mind, but we have not even tried to exercise fully the potential of our hearts and of our souls. This we knew to do in the past, but today sentiment, love, morality, understanding, humility and compassion are concepts which are usually derided in political and intellectual circles. The soul too has shrunk. Spirituality has been segregated from most government, public institutions and education. Finally, I am sorry to say, most of us have forgotten the good habit of saying "thanks" to You.

When I was a little boy, I remember that we had in our dining room the reproduction of a beautiful painting which showed a peasant and his wife in a field praying in the morning at sunrise when the bells were striking. It reminded the children in every home of France that we had to give thanks to You for all the blessings of this earth. When French peasants walked by a wheat field, they took off their caps. Bread was blessed by the father before being broken. Today, this has disappeared from many homes. I seldom see *The Angelus* of Millet any more and for years I have not seen anyone make the sign of the cross on a loaf of bread.

But in this beautiful square in Dallas, a new movement has begun. The dream of restoring gratitude in the world is becoming true. It is an idea whose time has come.

You know, dear Creator, again when I remember my youth, another image often comes back to me. At that time cars often stalled or would slide down the shoulders of the road, and we children were often called to help push them back onto the road. There came a point when we got tired and so we would place a stone or a block of wood behind the wheels. Then we looked proudly back at the distance we had covered. This is what the world must also do. This is what each individual must do. We must count our blessings. We must take inventory of what we have achieved. We must look back, be grateful and then look up at the rest of the road. This is why this world center was created. It must become a world movement, a spiral of the heart and of the soul outreaching for all leaders, educators, media, world servers and people, reminding them that above all we must be grateful to You for what we have received. Each of us in his own way and all together, we must help achieve an unprecedented destiny and fulfillment of the miracle of life on our wonderful planet. To do this, our friends of Thanksgiving Square have committed their help.

Dear God, I pray that we should be able here in this chapel to report to You each year on further progress of the human family, to strike out from our liabilities wars, conflicts, injustices, hatred, dishonesty and prejudice, and to add to our assets new friendships, more love, more world cooperation and a greater recognition of the miracle of life in the incomprehensible, vast universe.

Thank You, O God, for our little planet so rich with life, light, warmth, beauty, dream, invention, history, diversity and future. Thank You, O God, for the prodigy of life. My heart is smiling at the thought of all Your gifts. Thank You, dear God, thank You very much.

13

To Reach Peace, Teach Peace

Soon after his elevation to the pontificate, an event which took place during the International Year of the Child, Pope John Paul II sent his first message to governments and to heads of international organizations. It was entitled: "To Reach Peace, Teach Peace."

No theme could have been more timely. Indeed, the International Year of the Child obliged us to reflect collectively, nationally and individually about the conditions into which children are born today and the kind of future which is being prepared for them in various regions of the world. Also, it was a year of profound rethinking and activity in the field of world education. From various walks of life and regions of the world, news reaches us of mounting dissatisfaction with the way children are being taught about our planet and its peoples. Many schools and universities are turning to the United Nations for help in improving their curricula. From Peru comes the suggestion for an International Year for Global Education. The methods of teaching and the curricula of the UN international schools are attracting wide attention, and university students are turning their high, almost fascinated hopes towards the United Nations University in Tokyo and the University of Peace in Costa Rica.

Pope John Paul II's message dealt with many aspects of the subject, including linguistics, from which he would like to see eradicated concepts and language perpetuating hatred, conflict, division and war. Two aspects are particularly important to world servers: one is the necessity to convey to the children and peoples the right knowledge about this world; the second is the necessity to teach them the right attitude.

Teaching the Right Knowledge

Each human being is born into this world with given senses, a physiology and a genetic legacy which epitomize the entire past evolution of humankind in our planetary conditions. His life will be the result of the interplay of his aptitudes with his physical and human environment. He is literally "led out of ignorance" (*e-ducare*) by the family, school, religion, higher education and, last but not least, by life itself. Generation after generation, humanity's total growing knowledge is genetically and socially transmitted to a constantly renewed and expanding stream of human life.

One of the most crucial questions facing humanity at the present juncture of its evolution is whether we do convey the right information and knowledge about our planet and its people to the four and a half billion human beings alive, especially to the newcomers, the children. Such knowledge falls basically into three categories: the earth, humanity and the individual human person.

As regards *the earth*, humanity has made incredible progress in knowlege of our globe and its exact place in the universe, our relations with the sun, outer space, our atmosphere, biosphere, our seas and oceans, our land masses, our arable land, the planet's water, its mineral and energy resources, our vegetal and animal world, the inside of the earth's crust, down to the infinitesimally small world of the atom, of particles, of the cell, of genes, of microbiology. Yes, it is a prodigious scientific image which reaches the United Nations through its thirty-two specialized agencies and global programs. As a result we can educate our children as we have never done before about our little but so miraculously rich, life-teeming planet circling in the vast universe. We can show them an astonishingly beautiful, well-ordered tapestry of human knowledge, from the infinitely large to the infinitely small, as no Galileo, no Newton, no Copernicus would ever have dreamed possible.

My only misgiving is that rarely do schools and universities mention the world institutions in which the synthesis of this knowledge converges and in which the great tapestry is being woven. Where are the schools of this world which teach the young about the UN's work and major world conferences on outer space, on the seas and oceans, the world's climate, food, water, the deserts, science and technology, the atom, etc.? Where is the child who could name a few of the world's specialized agencies? Only UNICEF and the UN's Stockholm Conference on the Environment are known to any extent in the schools. We are thus missing a great opportunity to reassure the children and the people that governments are beginning to work together on an unprecedented scale to know, monitor, protect and manage our planetary home better.

Similarly, when it comes to knowledge about *the human family*, we have made great progress: we know how many we are, where we are, how many children, men and women, adults and elderly we are; we know that there are four hundred and fifty million handicapped, five hundred million malnourished and not far from a billion illiterates; we know how long we can expect to live in various parts of the world. No major aspect of the human family has been neglected during these last few decades: we had Economic Development Conferences, a World Population Conference, a Youth Conference, a World Assembly on Aging; UNICEF is looking after the children; the Human Settlements Conference has surveyed our location and migrations; there were two World Women's Conferences; there was an International Year of Disabled Persons; there were vast efforts and a World Conference on Racism, and so on and so forth. But again, not enough is being taught to the children about our knowledge of the exact and often so unjust and disparate conditions of the human family on our planet, or about the objectives humanity seeks to attain.

The situation is even worse when it comes to the groups into which humanity has been divided by history: the group into which a child is born is often presented to him as being superior to the totality. A nation is shown to be greater than humanity, a language greater than human communication, a race better than others, an ideology or political system superior to others, a culture or history more glorious than others, a religious rite more valuable than universal spirituality, a corporation as the greatest, and so forth and so on. It is especially from these struggles among groups that conflicts and wars originate. This is indeed one of the greatest problems of our time, an anthropology or social biology which still remains to be written, studied and resolved: what are the reasons for this phenomenon, why is it that the supreme interests of the entire human family are so difficult to recognize, to organize and to respect, how can the innumerable groups on this planet be made to work together in peace, harmony and common purpose, without arms, waste and risks of endangering the entire life of our globe? These problems have not yet found an answer, and we can therefore not reproach educators for not educating children in the right way. All we can do, for the moment, is to teach that recourse to war and violence must be eliminated from group relations. This is the first preliminary step towards peace and disarmament. And when we look back at the eradication of slavery on this planet, at the progress achieved in racial equality and equality of men and women, there is good hope that we will also solve sooner or later the problems of economic and social injustice, and of peace and war. There can be very little doubt about it.

Thirdly, when it comes to *the human person*, that alpha and omega of all our efforts—endowed with the miracle of life—we should also show the child the good progress achieved and the distance still to be covered. Humanity is expending countless efforts to know better and improve the physical and mental life of the human person, but greater attention must also be given to the moral and spiritual aspects of life. The worlds of morality, of feelings, of introspection and spirituality lag far and unnecessarily behind the colossal advances of science and technology. In the United Nations, humanity has written in common one of the greatest sets of philosophical documents ever: the Declaration and Covenants on Human Rights, including those of disadvantaged groups. Here we have an official, world recognition of the miracle each human life represents in the universe, the care, respect, dignity and treatment it demands. The philosophy of this planet's four and a half billion individual human lives, including the child's right to economic, social, moral and spiritual development, has been largely written in the United Nations. Alas, in how many schools of this earth are these human rights being taught? Would it not be an immense progress towards peace, and justice if each child of this planet were taught about the Universal Declaration of Human Rights? What more beautiful charter could there be for our world social relations than these words:

All human beings are born free and equal in dignity and rights. They are endowed with reason and conscience and should act towards one another in a spirit of brotherhood.

To complete the general sketch of a right global, planetary education, one would need to add the time dimension, from the eternity of the universe to the infinitesimal life span of an atomic particle, from the four and a half billion years of our past to the six to eight billion years of our future, the three million years of human evolution, our climatic past and future, the histories and futures of languages, cultures, beliefs and human groups, the life span of the human person in all this emerging, grandiose picture of the universe, our being the product of all past and a building block to all future, and the rules and responsibilities deriving therefrom for each of us. The correct time framework of education still leaves much to be desired. We could learn immensely from the religions, which have always seen the human person as part of the universe and of all time, his total physical, mental, moral and spiritual dimension as a unique, unrepeatable convergence of infinity and eternity.

Teaching the Right Attitude

Pope John Paul II starts his message as follows:

> The great cause of peace between the peoples needs all the energies of peace present in man's heart. It was to the releasing and cultivation of these energies—to the training of them—that my predecessor Paul VI decided, shortly before his death, that the 1979 World Day of Peace should be dedicated: "TO REACH PEACE, TEACH PEACE."

This is another fundamental requirement for the peace and further progress of human civilization on our planet. We must want and work with all our hearts and strength for peace and the fulfillment of the miracle of life for all. Without such will we shall fail; with it, we will succeed. There is a mysterious yet unexplained choice in individual as well as in collective life: we can abandon, be pessimistic and give in to despair, thus setting the stage for our own defeat and downfall, or we can throw down our gauntlet for life, for success and progress, thus bringing into full play the mysterious and miraculous forces and aptitudes for life transmitted to us at birth. This will, this attitude is not the end product of logic or thinking alone; it is a vital drive which sustains life in the complex mysteries around us in a forever incomprehensible but marvelous universe. Without it, our individual lives, a group, a civilization, a culture and humanity perish. Nothing therefore is more important than teaching children the right attitude towards life, peace and human progress. All great religions have placed the miracle of faith at the center of human progress. This is no less true today. Nothing would be more damaging to human peace and ascent than to believe that it cannot be done, that peace, justice and survival are unlikely or impossible.

In this connection, these beautiful words by Teilhard de Chardin are particularly appropriate:

> Let us not forget that faith in peace is not possible, not justifiable, except in a world dominated by faith in the future, *faith in Man* and the progress of Man. By this token, so long as we are not all of one mind, and with a sufficient degree of ardour, it will be useless for us to seek to draw together and unite. We shall only fail.
>
> That is why, when I look for reassurance as to our future, I do not turn to official utterances, or "pacifist" manifestations, or conscientious objectors. I turn instinctively towards the ever more numerous institutions and associations of men where in the search for knowledge a new spirit is silently taking shape around us—the soul of Mankind resolved at all costs to achieve, in its total integrity, the uttermost fulfillment of its powers and its destiny.[1]

It is true, humanity's piercing of the surrounding reality and its intervention as a factor of new, man-made complexities are at the source of much of today's anxiety. But the complexity and mystery of life are not worse now than they were for primitive man. For him it was an even more threatening and incomprehensible world. And we, like him, have at our disposal the great simplifying syntheses translated into human language: belief, beauty, goodness, love, peace, happiness, harmony, wisdom, knowledge, etc.—in other words, all the light, bright and positive sides of life instead of the dark, disintegrating and negative ones.

Hence, the enlightened self-interest and imperative to be optimistic, to bring into play *the miracle of faith*, to release the forces of the heart and of the soul in the largest number of people.

It is with human society as it is with the individual: we need a vision, an objective, a shore to swim towards. If not, we will drown. Life needs to be believed in, to be sustained and nourished. Hence it is our paramount duty to educate children in the art of living and happiness, in believing in humanity's success and in the establishment of a peaceful, just, brotherly and happy world.

All great prophets, visionaries and reformers understood the central importance of education. One of them said: "Give me your children, and I will give you the world." Today we should say: "Give

[1] Teilhard de Chardin, *The Future of Man* (New York: Harper Colophon Books, 1975), p. 159.

the children the right view of the world and they will give us peace."
The time has come when we must reform our curricula, reorder our
knowledge, honestly and objectively, into a vast synthesis which will
show our exact place in the universe and in time and the means of
our progress from a troubled past into a peaceful future. Yes, above
all, our first task is to put order in our knowledge, and from the
magnificent picture which will emerge will flow an immense respect
for creation and the imperative necessity for peace, justice and
fulfillment for all.

Secondly, we must re-establish the unity of science and sentiment,
knowledge and faith, the arts, humanities and spirituality, the inner
world and the outer world, in a search for the total flowering of the
human person.

Third, we must believe in peace, human ascent and justice. As for
all things on this earth, a period of preparation, of take-off is needed.
This is typically the case for economic development, and the same is
true for peace, disarmament and world-wide cooperation. The beginnings are slow, but suddenly a progress which seemed so difficult,
nay, impossible, begins to gain momentum. Proper global education
is an essential factor towards such progress and it should include
teaching the children about the instruments of peace and the first
universal organization ever on this planet: the United Nations and
its family of agencies.

Humanity has been seized by a vast, evolutionary mutation which
will permit us to progress towards both greater unity and more diversity, to understand the vast distances of the universe and the world
of the infinitely small, to grasp our position between all past and all
future, to become the responsible managers and caretakers of our
planet, and to fulfill human nature to an unprecedented extent in
all its aspects—physical, mental, moral and spiritual. We live in a
great moment in evolution. Like Darwin in the last sentence of *The
Origin of Species*, one is tempted to exclaim:

> . . . whilst this planet has gone cycling on according to the fixed
> law of gravity, from so simple a beginning endless forms most beauti-
> ful and most wonderful have been and are being evolved.

Yes, a new form of humanity most beautiful and most wonderful
is being evolved right under our eyes.

PART III

The Global Transcendence
of Religions

14

An Appeal to World Religions for Peace[1]

I would like to outline to this great gathering of religious leaders the following elements of hope in the world situation as I see them emerge in the United Nations, so that when you return to your countries you might help consolidate these trends which in my view will change the world and lead sooner or later to the type of society humans have been dreaming of for thousands of years. Among these positive elements I would like to single out the following:

First, during the last few centuries and especially since World War II, our world has finally appeared to us for what it has always been: *a global world*. For two or more million years we have lived on this planet not even knowing that it was a sphere! If our globe could speak, he would say to us:

"I pity you humans! You make me laugh! I have been rotating and circling around the sun for four and a half billion years! I have witnessed many upheavals in my flesh. I have seen continents and ice covers come and go, seas change place, mountains emerge, an atmosphere be born, vegetation arise, life develop and species evolve and disappear. You came into being only two million years ago. I have seen you crawl in utter ignorance for most of that time. Only a few hundred years ago did you at long last discover America and that I was round! And only a few years ago did you see me in my totality from outer space. I have been observing you and I want to tell you this:

"You will go nowhere if you do not remember that I will be around for several more billion years; that my body will be shaken

[1] Transcript of an address before the Third World Conference on Religion and Peace, United Nations and Princeton, August–September 1980.

by more climatic changes; that for your maximum happiness and survival you must treat and manage me with care; that you must increasingly put yourselves in my place and lift your eyes, as I do, to the sun, to the universe, to infinity and eternity of which we are only a part. After your cave age, after your tribal age, after your feudal age, after your national age, you have at long last entered *my* age: the global age. But this is still insufficient, for you have yet to enter the cosmic or divine age and see your proper place in the fathomless universe and time. You still have to become the planet of God."

And we could justifiably answer our globe: "Yes, it took us a long time, but we are there. Haven't you seen us lately make our world a global, interdependent unit through science, technology and expanding human relations? Haven't you noticed our satellites which are observing you, studying you, and linking every point of your body with others through communications? Thousands of airplanes and ships circle you. Tens of thousands of meetings and congresses are being held on your crust. We peoples of the world have never known each other so well. Our society is being more closely interwoven every day in thousands of ways into a vast interdependent, global unit. Do you think that all this will be without effects?"

And we could add another great sign of this new age and historical trend: the birth of the United Nations itself. Yes, we should never forget that the ancient dream to have a universal organization has at long last come true. I am astonished that all peoples of the earth do not rejoice at that achievement which all the great prophets, visionaries, philosophers and humanists had been dreaming of. Yes, all nations of this planet are now meeting, learning from each other and beginning to cooperate in many world agencies and programs dealing with practically every problem under the sun. How happy the Gautama Buddha, Jesus and Mahomet would be if they could see the United Nations! This is why Pope Paul VI when he visited the UN described his trip as "the end of a journey that started two thousand years ago." For the first time the dream of the Catholic (Universal) Church was fulfilled: its Pope could speak to the Assembly of all nations of earth. He asked therefore in moving terms for the support of the United Nations: "Our message is first of all a moral and solemn ratification of this lofty institution . . . convinced as we are that it represents the obligatory path of modern civilization and world peace." And Pope John Paul II after his resounding visit to the United Nations, when he left, repeated several times, with tears in his eyes, looking back at the UN buildings: "God bless the United Nations, God bless the United Nations."

Hence the need for all world religions to actively support and thoroughly explain the United Nations to their peoples, for it is here that the old dreams of humanity for peace, non-violence, disarmament, justice, world ethics and human dignity find their latest expression. This is most important, so that this organization shall never be allowed to die or to disappear but be strengthened and enlightened in the cause of human ascent. As Pope Paul VI rightly said: "This edifice that you have built must never fall again into ruins. It must be improved upon and adapted to the demands which the history of the world will make upon it." This is the new ecumenical spirit which is needed. As someone who has worked in the world organization for over thirty years, who knows it inside out from its good and its weak sides, I can only say this: it is the beginning of the fulfillment of one of the most prodigious dreams of humanity. It is the greatest hope we ever had in our divided, conflictual journey on planet Earth. We must make it work. We must help the dream come true with all our strength, all our mind, all our heart and all our soul. We need the support and the prayers of the people. We cannot win if the people do not plead with their leaders for the support and strengthening of the UN. This is the first great hopeful element which all of us can foster and nourish in order to achieve a peaceful and better world. And your help can be invaluable.

A second positive element is that we have become a new, transcended species with vastly expanded capacities, senses, knowledge and dominion over our planetary home. We were born into our particular planetary conditions with very limited senses and capacities. We have been able to achieve a tremendous miracle: that of extending practically every sense and capacity in every direction. Our eyesight did not reach more than a few kilometers, but we are now able, thanks to science and technology, to look into the far expanses of the universe, to take pictures of stars which are billions of light-years away. We can see into the infinitely small through electronic microscopes and picoscopes and observe the behavior of nuclear particles and subparticles in atomic bubble chambers. We can now hear the sounds of the universe through radio and a voice from New Delhi in New York through satellite communications. The short range of our legs has been multiplied by airplanes and other swift means of transportation. We can cross the seas, fly in the air and circle the globe in space capsules. The capacity of our brain has been multiplied thousands of times through computers and electronic devices. We have extended the capacity of our hands through incredible machines and factories. Thus, we are a new transcended species which has explored thoroughly the little corner of the universe which we occupy, and lifted our eyes vastly into the infinite.

We have made much less progress in expanding and transcending our hearts and souls, our morality and our spirituality. The great human achievements of the last few centuries have been principally in the domains of matter and mind. We have not even tried to explore what humanity could achieve if it transcended also its moral and spiritual capacities. This page has still to be written. We are only at the beginning of it. We can witness the birth of a morality in the United Nations, but immorality in this world by far still outweighs morality. Think alone of the five hundred and fifty billion dollars which are spent each year on insane, life-annihilating armaments while there are so many poor. We are still at the cave age of establishing right human relations on this planet. We have been able to look at the stars with gigantic telescopes, but has this species honestly tried to lift its heart and soul to the universe? Have we tried to become not only a global family but a spiritual family, standing in awe before the beautiful, stupendous creation? Have we really asked ourselves the fundamental question: what is this little planet in the universe and what is our purpose and destiny on it? Must we not see ourselves as a meaningful part of total creation and of the total stream of time? These are the great questions which political leaders must ask themselves. In the United Nations they have been raised very forcefully by Dag Hammarskjöld and U Thant. This again is a positive trend. Humanity, despite innumerable wars, accidents, errors and foolishness, has been able during the two million years of its story to maintain an ever ascending course. It stands today at an infinitely higher level than ever before. It is our task to bring it to even higher summits. This is where the religions have a fundamental role to play. They can coalesce, mobilize their people and demand from governments that morality and spirituality be put on a par with scientific and technological development. This is one of the greatest blessings that could happen to humanity. Otherwise science, technology and world cooperation will remain fraught with much immorality, because their ethics have been insufficiently defined. We are only at the beginning of a world ethics. In the upward march of humanity, religions can play a momentous role. They can help humanity's political progress to transcend itself into the realms of morality and love which all great prophets heralded as the ultimate key to the problem of peace on earth. Above all, religions can help humanity better understand its right place and behavior in creation. When it comes to the mystical, extraterrestrial comprehension of the universe, religions are far ahead of science and technology, of governments and of the United Nations.

A third positive element in the world situation is that, as a result of the improvement of our senses through science and technology, we have been able for the first time ever in our evolution to draw a very simple, magnificent Copernican tapestry of all our knowledge of the surrounding physical and living world. This picture has emerged from the work of the UN agencies where all human knowledge converges. Our human race has now a prodigious view which reaches from the infinitely large to the infinitesimally small. It all falls into place. We are hanging and twirling in the universe around our sun on a given planet endowed with specific resources. We have looked at this planet from every possible angle. We have examined it, investigated it globally in a whole series of resounding world conferences. Every segment, every global aspect of our little planet has been examined world-wide. Historians someday will consider these years as a crucial turning point in evolution. As a result, for the first time, we possess a great encyclopedia of knowledge which shows us that our planet is a very special one, that it is a magnificent abode in the universe compared with so many other lifeless planets. Perhaps we are one of the luckiest celestial bodies. Perhaps the religions are right when they think that God has a special design for us. As a result, we have great responsibilities towards this lovely globe of ours. Religions are not particularly inclined towards science. This is an error, for the knowledge of this marvelous picture of creation is part of our spiritual journey.

The fourth element is no less dramatic: in recent years, humanity has not only appraised its entire planet, but it has also for the first time taken full cognizance of itself. This had never happened before. For the first time, the human race has studied, analyzed and measured itself. As recently as thirty years ago we did not even know how many people lived on this planet! Today we know how many we are, how many women and men there are, how many children, handicapped and old people there are, and what our future numbers are likely to be. Every single global aspect of the human condition, be it longevity, nutrition, literacy, the state of health, standards of life, has been examined in world conferences or in one of the UN specialized agencies. UN demographers can tell us how long people can expect to live country by country. The International Labor Organization tells us how many unemployed people there are. The Food and Agriculture Organization tells us that there are still five hundred million hungry people. All this was totally unknown only a mere three decades ago. There were not even any world statistics at the time when I joined the United Nations! There had never been any world conferences or international years on this planet. This is all happening for the first time in our two million years of evolution. Religions here again have an important contribution to make because of their long experience and knowledge with social and human problems, from childhood to death.

A fifth positive element is the sudden increase in our time perception. It is only recently that humanity really began to think about its future. In 1945 we worked from year to year. Today governments and the entire United Nations system are geared to thinking and working decades ahead. The year 2000 is the normal time span for practically every UN agency. There is a world food plan 2000, a world health plan 2000, a world literacy plan 2000, a Third UN Economic Development Decade. The human species is extending its time dimension to a tremendous extent. This is another great victory of humanity, for as we expand our time vision we discover that our planet has limits and that certain things have become impossible. We encounter limits to growth, limits to resources, limits to human longevity, limits to the life-bearing capacity of our planet. It is increasingly important for us to see our place not only in the total planet but also in the total stream of time. Here again, the religions have a great contribution to make. While governments and international organizations speak in terms of a few decades, the religions have always seen humanity in the total time frame of the universe. There is no religion that does not see life from creation to the apocalypse. What the astrophysicists tell us today about the birth of a solar system, its multibillion-year-long stability and its ultimate collapse, only to be reborn in the form of another star, is known to all major religions by instinct, by vision. Hence the religions have an invaluable experience, for they see the human race in a much more complete, integral relationship with eternity than the scientists, economists and developers of today. The religions possess the right instinct about our place in total time. Their perceptions can be of utmost importance to scientists and political men.

Finally, there is another recent discovery which the religions knew from the beginning and have been relentlessly advocating, even if their competition over this fundamental truth led to many unfortunate religious wars and behavior contrary to their beliefs: the tremendous worth, dignity and sanctity of each individual human life. The more scientists study the human person, the more they discover that it is a true miracle. No human being has ever existed before in exactly the same form and will never exist again in the same form in all eternity. Even if this were the case, the circumstances of his life would be different. So we discover that each life is unique, that each human being is an incredibly complex and marvelous entity in the infinity of cosmoses, from the infinitely large to the infinitely small, linked with all matter, elements and life, yet endowed with his own, astonishing identity. We are thus given a tremendous view of the universe in which everything is linked and yet is an entity, from a galaxy and a star to an atomic particle. We know how unique, how sacred and how soulful a member of our own family is. We know it especially at the moment of death. The same is true of every member of the human family. As a result, a human should never be killed and should never kill. He should never be harmed and never harm. He should never inflict violence or have violence be inflicted on him.

Around this view of the uniqueness and preciousness of human life turns the whole story of human rights and of the establishment of peaceful and right human relations on this planet. It is the cornerstone of the coming global civilization and an absolute confirmation of what the religions have been saying for thousands of years. Isn't it obvious therefore that the religions and the United Nations should form a great alliance in the defense of human life, so that finally peace and the sanctity and dignity of the human person will become world-wide realities in our planetary home?

These are some of the main positive trends which can be seen from the vantage point of the United Nations. Despite their idiosyncrasies, errors, reluctance and misbehavior, nations are learning their lessons and the world is changing. The human race is seeking its planetization with unprecedented intensity. The old battles of humans with the elements and with each other will soon come to an end through very fundamental and powerful imperatives of evolution. The next stage will be our entry into a moral global age—the global age of love—and a global spiritual age—the cosmic age. We are now moving fast towards the fulfillment of the visions of the great prophets who through cosmic enlightenment saw the world as one unit, the human race as one family, sentiment as the cement of that family and the soul as our link with the universe, eternity and God. As Kant said:

"The star-studded sky above us and moral consciousness in us."

This is the message I would like you to take home to your people. Ask them to cherish their United Nations, to have faith and to pray for us.

15

Pope Paul VI's Doctrine of Peace

During my many years with the United Nations, I had occasion to observe the important role of Pope Paul VI in world affairs and matters of peace. He was a dear friend of former Secretary-General U Thant, whom I often heard speak of him with great fondness and admiration. Pope Paul was one of the few people, a group of very special persons, with whom U Thant was in constant spiritual communion. Later I had the privilege of accompanying Secretary-General Waldheim to Rome when he visited the Holy Father for the first time. I can remember vividly how large the issue of peace loomed in the spirit and heart of His Holiness. There is no doubt that Paul VI, together with John XXIII and John Paul II, will be remembered as the three great Popes of Peace, pioneers of a momentous transcendence of the Catholic Church into the New Age.

I have read much of what Paul VI wrote and said about human values and peace. His thoughts, writings and pronouncements constitute a unique doctrine of peace for our time. I hope that scholars and political scientists will bring out someday the richness, depth, vision and timeliness of that doctrine. Let us not forget that the Catholic Pope, like the Secretary-General of the UN, is a global, ecumenic man who has the whole world and its people at heart.[1] His thoughts and actions are therefore of utmost importance to the world community.

The following are a few comments on some of Pope Paul VI's fundamental ideas. They are based primarily on the remarkable an-

[1] Dag Hammarskjöld once observed that there were two Popes on this planet: a spiritual Pope in Rome and a civilian Pope in New York, namely, the Secretary-General of the UN.

nual messages issued by him on the occasion of the Day of Peace on January 1, which he instituted and which is always a very special event for the United Nations.

Pacts Must Be Observed

One of the cardinal principles in the Pope's doctrine is that pacts must be observed (*pacta servanda sunt*). This is the central theme of his message for 1976, "Real Weapons of Peace." How familiar it sounds to the minds of the delegates to the United Nations! Personally, I came to the conclusion long ago that the single most important way to achieve universal peace would be the strict observance of the United Nations Charter and the solemn pledge never to break it under any circumstances, which is, alas, not the case. Governments, when they break the Charter for selfish reasons, always think that they break it only a little bit. In reality they break it entirely and make the international system of security unworkable and untrustworthy. The Charter, it cannot be repeated often enough, is one of the most remarkable pacts of all times. It contains all necessary principles, methods, procedures and rules of conduct to prevent conflicts and to ensure peaceful relations among nations. A full, universal, honest, unreserved and painstaking adherence to its spirit and provisions by all members would make it the most effective instrument of peace ever. This in turn would forge the conditions under which nations would entrust their security to their collective organization rather than to arsenals of weapons or the armed protective wings of powerful tutors and military alliances.

Peace Depends on You Too

How right the Holy Father was when in his 1974 message he recalled this fundamental truth of human society. Peace is not the sole matter of governments and international agencies. Peace is the matter of every human being. In the end, total peace, justice, understanding and happiness in the world can only be the sum total of the peace, justice, understanding and happiness of all individuals, families, cities, nations, races, continents and cultures. Peace is interdependent in time and in space. The sense of peace, justice and understanding of a statesman may have been taught to him as a child by his parents, by the example of a public leader or by a good teacher. And the world may benefit immensely from that circumstance if, at a moment of crisis, that leader extends his hands to his neighbor instead of seizing arms. A single act of peace is never lost. It has mysterious, far-reaching effects in the total world fabric.

There rests an immense power for peace in the four and a half billion inhabitants of earth. People can be the masters of world peace if they work for it, if they insist on it, if they take an interest in their first universal institutions and give them their strength, their minds, their hearts and their spirits, a fact to which no government can remain insensitive. Thus, nothing in my view could do more for the strengthening and effectiveness of the United Nations than a good understanding, knowledge and wholehearted support by the public. Peace or war may depend on it. Generation after generation will have to be educated in matters of peace and global living, if peace is to become a permanent feature of this planet.

Disarmament

His Holiness repeatedly insisted on disarming as the primary condition for peace. Whatever justifications a state or group of states may have for resorting to armaments for their security, no universal person or institution can ever lend support to the idea of a planet of armed nations. From the standpoint of the earth, armaments are a folly, a disgrace and an intolerable waste. They are a folly when one thinks of the type of insane, life-annihilating weapons which are being master-minded and accumulated on our fragile globe, in the air, on the soil, in the soil, on the seas and in the seas. They are a disgrace, for they cast a severe doubt on human intelligence and on the validity of the earth's present political system. They are an intolerable waste when one thinks that five hundred and fifty billion dollars are being squandered each year on armaments—the equivalent of total world expenditures on health and education—when so many hundreds of millions of human beings cry out for food, medical care, schools and shelter on our planet. As the Pope once remarked, armaments kill, even if they are not used: they kill scores of children and people who could have been saved from hunger, malnutrition and malady.

The scandal has reached such proportions that renewed attempts at disarming are being incessantly launched by the United Nations. Even if there is little chance for early world disarmament, this must be repeated time and again, and it must remain one of the first priorities of the United Nations. There is even more reason to eradicate armaments from this planet than there was to eradicate smallpox. All conceivable files and proposals for disarmament are ready. They have been painstakingly worked out over the last three decades. All depends on the will of the peoples and nations, especially the big nations who bear the main responsibility in this matter.

If You Want Peace, Work for Justice

How pertinent are these words chosen by His Holiness for the title of his peace message in 1972! Injustice is one of the main arguments adduced by its victims to justify and advocate violence and war. The idea of a "holy" or "just" violence has not yet been eradicated from the mind of man. When utter despair sets in, it takes a saint not to think of violence and rebellion as a means of achieving justice. How can we envisage a peaceful, brotherly world, for example, if the fantastic injustices between rich and poor are allowed to prevail on our planet? The drafters of the Charter saw it most clearly when they considered economic and social progress to be one of the main foundations of peace. We see this also when attempts are being made to stem such new forms of international violence as hijacking, the taking of hostages and terrorism. The perpetrators often tell us that, despairing of finding a peaceful solution to such problems as independence, crying social and economic inequalities or the regaining of a homeland, they have no other ways but violence. We can have no illusion: the problem of world justice has been clearly and forcefully placed before states and the United Nations. Its definition and attainment represent one of the most staggering world-wide challenges of our time.

Promotion of Human Rights

In "Promotion of Human Rights, the Road to Peace" (1969 message), again His Holiness touched on one of the fundamental causes of discontent and conflict on our planet. The United Nations is often criticized for not doing enough in this field. In my opinion, historians looking back someday at the last decades of our century will recognize that the United Nations' definition of the inalienable rights of the human person has been one of the greatest collective philosophical achievements of humankind.

The question here again is one of faithful and strict compliance by governments. Much remains to be done in this respect, but at least the world community is on the right track, despite considerable difficulties stemming from divergent views regarding the position of the individual within the various social and political groups of which he is part. With time and persistence, all violations of human rights will have the same fate as slavery and racism.

Consciousness of Human Brotherhood

In his 1971 message, His Holiness reminded us forcefully of the basic truth that "Every man is my brother." Nothing, indeed, in the long run will contribute more to the forging of a peaceful and orderly society than the recent emergence of a true world-wide community. Prophets and philosophers had all perceived the fundamental unity and brotherhood of humans, but for the first time in all our long journey such a community is now being truly born. This is due primarily to the tremendous strides in science and technology which have revealed the immensely complex natural interdependence of everything on earth and have promoted over a short few decades a no less astoundingly dense and irreversible network of man-made interdependencies. Willingly or not, no nation desirous of surviving in these circumstances can afford not to pray and work for peace. This is our greatest chance of all times. One can see it well at the United Nations, where behind protracted political difficulties and idiosyncrasies the human community is fashioning an unprecedented system of world agencies and instrumentalities which play a vital role in the probing, monitoring and assessment of our total planetary home as well as in the guidance of human behavior and destiny in it. In my view, the numerous UN agencies, world conferences, meetings and endeavors are a direct, most concrete biological manifestation of the nascent efforts of the human species to establish itself as one interdependent, fulfilled and peaceful community in harmony with its planetary ecosystem.

If You Want Peace, Defend Life

In his 1976 message His Holiness dealt with the ultimate goal of all our efforts: the defense of life. In the great universal school of philosophy which the United Nations has become, it is more and more apparent that humanity is setting the highest objectives ever for human life. Priority has been given first to the attainment of a good physical life for all, in terms of food, health and shelter, and of a decent mental life through education, without which there can be neither dignity nor understanding of the miracle of life. In those countries where these two objectives have been attained, people in increasing numbers, especially youth, are demanding a new dimension of life: they insist on the establishment of a moral society, the right not to kill, not to wear arms, and the establishment of morality, honesty, trust and integrity in all walks of life, public and private. This trend has emerged in the UN where more and more codes of ethics and rules of conduct are being requested on subjects as diverse as biological engineering, the comportment of the police, the transfer of technology, and transnational corporations.

Everything is beginning to fall into place. We have acquired during the last few years a remarkable knowledge of all major global conditions of our planet. The challenge is now whether harmonious cooperation can be established between all social and political groups so that each human being, this miracle of creation and unique cosmos, will be able to achieve full consciousness of life—physical, mental, moral and spiritual. Yes, if we want peace, the first step is to defend life and to realize its uniqueness, sanctity, inalienability, sovereignty and miraculous character.

* * *

The Pope's rich doctrine of peace evokes innumerable other thoughts and comments. May I simply join in His Holiness' optimism and belief in the human race. Yes, as he exclaimed, peace is possible. Yes, disarmament is possible. Yes, justice is possible. Yes, human dignity is possible. Yes, a planet of love is possible. We may stand on the threshold of one of the greatest periods ever in evolution, if follies and accidents can be prevented. Humanity's incredible achievements in the realms of science, technology and thought can now be matched also in the social, humanitarian, ethical, moral, political and spiritual fields. It is through the development of ties of sentiment, love, understanding, give and take, truth, altruism, compassion and global order, and through a full realization of the miracle of life, that we will be able to embark upon the next segment of our prodigious journey in evolution. Pope Paul's vision and doctrine of peace, which translate into modern terms the eternal message of

Christ, are luminous guideposts on our road to becoming the planet of God.

As Teilhard de Chardin announced:

The day will come when, after harnessing the ether, the winds, the tides, gravitation, we shall harness for God the energies of love. And, on that day, for the second time in the history of the world, man will have discovered fire.

16

The Visit of Pope John Paul II
to the United Nations

One day, after the session of the Economic and Social Council in Geneva, as I was prepared to leave for a visit to my relatives in Alsace-Lorraine, I received a phone call from Secretary-General Waldheim.

"Robert, you may know that I have invited Pope John Paul II to visit and address the United Nations. He has just accepted and will come to New York in October. I wish to appoint you as my personal representative to organize and coordinate the visit. Could you come on Sunday to my hotel for a first meeting with the Pope's representatives, who will be coming from Rome?"

That meant the end of our planned journey to my home region but also the beginning of one my most interesting assignments in the United Nations. The details, incidents and multifaceted aspects of that event could fill a separate volume, for the public has no idea how many delicate and fascinating problems such a visit involves. I will only mention a few of them, each a major headache:

— How much time would the Pope spend in the UN and what time would be left for New York City? (This raised considerable problems with the Archdiocese of New York.)
— Would it be a visit to the UN, as was Pope Paul VI's trip in 1965, or would it be a visit which would start on United States soil? (This raised major protocol problems.)
— Who would receive him at the airport, what authorities would

be allowed to greet him, to shake his hands and to make speeches?

— What security and what media coverage would there be at the airport?

— How would the cavalcade proceed from the airport to New York, what route would it follow, what traffic control and security arrangements would be made?

— Who would receive him at the entrance of the UN? Who would take the elevator with him? Who from the Vatican and from the cardinalate would accompany him?

— What exact timetable and route would he follow in the UN, minute by minute, including time to wash his hands?

— What heads of state and foreign ministers would he see, collectively or separately?

— How much time and talks would he have with the Secretary-General?

— The exchange of gifts and the taking of official photographs.

— Television arrangements with more than one hundred countries for the televising of the visit.

— The accommodation of three thousand journalists, six hundred of them accompanying the Pope from Rome; the issuance of passes to them and their stationing along the route taken by the Pontiff to and in the UN.

— The exposure of the UN staff to the Pope, including some sick members who wanted a healing benediction from him.

— The speeches he was to deliver to different audiences in five different rooms; their readiness and distribution in many languages, without any advance leakages to the press.

— Who would be admitted to the General Assembly Hall (a major headache)?

— How would the cardinals, the Pope's entourage, the distinguished guests, the press, the Catholic organizations, etc., be seated?

— Where and with whom would the Pope have luncheon?

— Who would be invited to the afternoon reception at which His Holiness would meet individually a long list of personalities, including all heads of state and ministers of foreign affairs present at the General Assembly, all ambassadors of the one hundred and fifty-four member nations and their wives, many New York guests and U.S. personalities?

— What final speeches would be delivered?
— Arrangements for the departure of the Pope.

And I could mention many, many other problems and headaches. Looking back at the event, I feel as though I exercised the function of a space flight director, who has to think of every possible detail and circumstance that might go wrong, or of a theater manager, who has to spend hundreds of hours on stage and backstage to provide the public with a smoothly running, perfect, beautiful two-hour show. Some of my friends asked me afterwards: "We didn't see you much on television among the people surrounding the Pope." Well, one doesn't see the space flight director and theater manager either!

Throughout the entire visit, until the very last moment, I was checking on details and potential mishaps. For example, while the official party of the Secretary-General went to receive the Pope at the airport, I was following a last time the Pontiff's itinerary at the UN, impersonating him and trying to find out if there could still be something that might go wrong. On that last rehearsal I found that two TV platforms, built during the night, were obstructing the route! I also discovered a lady who was placing tons of green plants on the platform where the Pope and the Secretary-General were to greet guests during the afternoon reception. I asked her:

"What on earth are you doing here?"

"I am the lady from the contracting firm which provides the flowers and green plants for UN receptions."

"Dear madam, not only is this platform going to look like a funeral scene, but do you see those platforms for TV and photographers across the room? They will take innumerable pictures and views of the guests being greeted by His Holiness, and each of the pictures is going to show palm leaves growing out of the head of the Pope, the Secretary-General and the guests! It will be a disaster. Could you remove all these tall plants and leave only a row of small flowerpots and plants?"

Thank God, all went well. A little before 6:00 P.M., Cardinal Cooke reappeared in his magnificent garments, ready to take delivery of his Pope. I handed His Holiness to him at 6:03, with only three minutes' delay and without any scratch or incident. I was physically and psychologically exhausted, happy that it was all over but also the proud possessor of a magnificent golden pectoral Crucifix given to me by His Holiness in appreciation of my efforts.

I apologize for all these details, which are only incidental to my subject, but I thought that they might be of some interest to the reader.

Regarding the substance and historical significance of the Pope's visit, I would have this to say:

First of all, any visit of the Pontiff of the Catholic Church is of utmost significance. One could trace the world's main historic events for the last two thousand years by studying the Popes' visits, non-visits, voluntary visits and forced visits away from Rome. Just remember the Pope's compelled visit to Rheims for the coronation of the Emperor Napoleon! Pope Paul VI inaugurated the Popes' modern visits around the world. Very symbolically and understandably, his first visit was to the poor: he visited Bombay for the International Eucharistic Congress. His next visit, at the invitation of U Thant, was to the community of nations in New York. He was so particular about that point that he did not even stay overnight on U.S. territory. Pope John Paul II changed that style and wanted to be exposed primarily to the people rather than to officialdom. But, for both, the UN was one of the most important, if not the most important, places on earth. As Pope Paul VI put it in his address to the General Assembly:

> "We have been journeying long and we bring with us a long history; we here celebrate the epilogue of a toilsome pilgrimage in search of a conversation with the entire world, from the day the commandment was given to us: 'Go and bring the good tidings to all peoples.' And it is you who represent all peoples."

Or in the words of John Paul II:

> As a universal community embracing the faithful belonging to almost all countries and continents, nations, peoples, races, languages and cultures, the Church is deeply interested in the existence and activity of the Organization whose very name tells us that it unites and associates nations and States. It unites and associates: it does not divide and oppose. This is the real reason, the essential reason, for my presence among you.

Secondly, on the occasion of Paul VI's visit, I was lucky to have been given by U Thant's family an unpublished text by the former Secretary-General covering a number of subjects which he had not treated in his memoirs. Among these was his invitation to Pope Paul VI to visit and address the United Nations.

Here are extracts from that text:

. . . Did I leave out anything of historical significance during my decade with the U.N. Secretariat? Yes, I must mention the historic visit of His Holiness Pope Paul VI to the United Nations on October 4, 1965. The story of my invitation and of the Pope's kind acceptance goes back to an event at Bombay on December 4, 1964.

The Pope had gone to Bombay to attend the International Eucharistic Congress. At a meeting with a group of journalists during his three-day stay in the Indian city, he addressed through them an appeal to the world. In part he said:

"We entrust to you Our special message to the world. Would that the nations could cease the armaments race, and devote their resources and energies instead to the fraternal assistance of the developing countries! Would that every nation, thinking thoughts of peace and not affliction and of war, would contribute even a part of its expenditure for arms to a great world fund for the relief of the many problems of nutrition, clothing, shelter and medical care which affect so many peoples!"

These words, coming from the head of a great religion, were in line with my own thoughts which I had expressed on several occasions. I had said repeatedly that the widening gulf between the rich and the poor countries was far more serious and ultimately far more explosive than the division of the world into East and West based on ideological differences. Moreover, I felt that the General Assembly Hall of the United Nations had been the forum for statesmen and politicians; economists and sociologists. From time to time why should not this great hall be the forum for spiritual and religious leaders? I discussed the idea of extending an invitation to His Holiness to address a special meeting of the General Assembly with the President of the 19th session of the General Assembly, Ambassador Alex Quaison-Sackey of Ghana. He was enthusiastic.

I immediately asked Pier Pasquale Spinelli, Under-Secretary and head of the European office of the United Nations at Geneva to sound out the Vatican confidentially if His Holiness would be agreeable to address the General Assembly if a formal invitation were to be sent to him. Mr. Spinelli, an Italian, and one of the wisest men who ever served the United Nations, made discreet soundings, and reported to me that if I were to extend an invitation, the reply would be affirmative.

And U Thant later in the text had this to say on the address of His Holiness to the General Assembly:

The scope of the speech covered the essential provisions of the United Nations Charter. He touched on themes which were also not in the Charter. "The edifice of modern civilization must be built on spiritual principles, which alone cannot only support it, but also illuminate and animate it," he said. As one who believes in the moral and spiritual development of man, I was deeply moved. In fact the Pope's visit to the United Nations was not only of symbolic significance, but his speech was of historic importance. It left a lasting impression on the assembled diplomats of all religious denominations.

Thirdly, as the reader can well imagine, there was a very considerable intellectual and political preparation for the Pope's visit. One can visualize all the consultations that took place at the Vatican to prepare the form and the contents of the visit, in particular the Pontiff's major address to the General Assembly and his four other speeches. Bishop Marcinkus, my counterpart at the Vatican, told me that he had a reproduction of Harry Anderson's famous painting, *The Prince of Peace*, showing Christ knocking at the UN building, placed on one of the itineraries of the Pope in the Vatican. He casually made the Pope stop in front of it and said to him: "This is what you are supposed to do in New York." I answered Marcinkus: "You are wrong. Jesus is already inside the UN building."

I myself was asked for my expectations from the Pope's visit, and this is what I said in an editorial in the *Diplomatic World Bulletin*:

I expect his visit to be a resounding expression of support and encouragement for the UN, at a time when this first universal organization meets with dangerous cynicism, misunderstanding and lack of faith, especially on the part of the media. The Pope's mere presence at the UN, even if he did not pronounce a word, will be of tremendous importance.

I expect the Pope in his address to the General Assembly to lift the hearts and minds of governments, to give them a vision of what the world can be and should be as we approach the bimillennium, and to renew our faith that humanity can fulfill its ancient dreams of peace, harmony, brotherhood and personal dignity.

I expect the Pope to add a spiritual dimension to the emerging world vision which today, of necessity, gives priority to the physical and mental well-being of humanity, but must also be extended to an understanding and appreciation of the miracle of human life and of our planet in the vast universe and stream of time.

I expect the Pope to lift the hearts of all international servants of the UN and of its specialized agencies and programs, so that this first group of human beings who come from all quarters of the world and who work together for the good of humanity can bring forth new visions in philosophy, sociology, ideology and spirituality centered on the UN's noble objective of "unity in diversity."

I expect the Pope's visit to be a great, moving event which would make the hearts of the world's four and a half billion people beat together for a moment.

I expect the Pope's visit to engender in many hearts a profound prayer for peace, for kindness, for human brotherhood and for the success of the world-serving United Nations.

Basically and foremost, the Pope came to the UN unimpressed and uninfluenced by anyone and delivered his own, deeply felt, unique message, the product of his entire life and most intimate thinking. With the exception of a few protocol and diplomatic niceties, his message was entirely written in his own hand. I know this very well: for purposes of the media, we tried to have him keep his speech to thirty minutes or to one hour sharp. He insisted on more time and obtained this compromise: the entire written text would be left intact, but he would refrain from reading certain parts of it to keep it down to one hour. Until the actual delivery, no one knew what he would delete, for I saw three of his aides follow the text frantically during the meeting, deleting from it what he had omitted.

What was the main message of the Pope? While peace had been the main theme of Pope Paul VI's address in 1965, human rights, or rather the sanctity, sacredness and centrality of the individual human person, was his main theme. His speech is a classic on the subject. It merits reading and rereading, and it continues to be quoted often in UN speeches. I really wish that someday a book containing the UN speeches of the two Popes and their yearly messages on the Day of Peace might be published for wide distribution. The result would be a kind of Bible for modern times. The two following quotations are illustrative of the speech:

> "The questions that concern your functions and receive your attention—as is indicated by the vast organic complex of institutions and activities that are part of or collaborate with the United Nations, especially in the fields of culture, health, food, labour, and the peaceful uses of nuclear energy—certainly make it essential for us *to meet in the name of man in his wholeness*, in all the fullness and manifold riches of his spiritual and material existence. . . .

> "Each one of you represents a particular State, system and political structure, but what you represent above all are *individual human*

beings; you are all *representatives of men and women, of practically all the people of the world,* individual men and women, communities and peoples who are living the present phase of their own history and who are also part of the history of humanity as a whole, each of them a subject endowed with dignity as a human person, with his or her own culture, experiences and aspirations, tensions and sufferings, and legitimate expectations. This relationship is what provides the reason for *all political activity,* whether national or international, for in the final analysis this activity comes *from man,* is exercised *by man* and is *for man.* And if political activity is cut off from this fundamental relationship and finality, if it becomes in a way its own end, it loses much of its reason to exist. Even more, it can also give rise to a specific alienation; it can become extraneous to man; it can come to contradict humanity itself. In reality, what justifies the existence of any political activity is service to man, concerned and responsible attention to the essential problems and duties of his earthly existence in its social dimension and significance, on which also the good of each person depends."

He of course, like Paul VI, reminded the world assembly of the imperative of the spiritual:

"The progress of humanity must be measured not only by *the progress of science and technology,* which shows man's uniqueness with regard to nature, but also and chiefly by *the primacy given to spiritual values* and by *the progress of moral life.*"

It is perhaps this central role of the human person in his thought and life which explains best the tremendous charisma of John Paul II. I observed him closely during his speeches and his encounters with individual persons: his "charm," or rather the love and liking people feel for him, is the product of his own love and concern for each individual human person, met alone or in a group. He "descends" to the person and to the group. He lives them. He senses the whole, total person or the soul of a group, and submits his entire being, mind, heart and soul, to the comprehension of that person or group, and what they expect from him in terms of help, healing, elevation, hope and inspiration. What lessons I learned from him during that short intensive day! Indeed, in our age, people are sufficiently educated and sophisticated to expect a leader to embody the teachings and morality he professes. They can no longer be fooled. They instinctively and unmistakenly feel the charisma, the honesty, the living embodiment of goodness, kindness and love in the master, in the good leader of people. This explains the resonance and irradiation of Pope John Paul II far beyond his Catholic flock. The people of this planet are thirsty for loving, good, ethical, moral, pure and disinterested leaders and public servants, for individuals whose hearts, minds, actions and souls unreservedly embrace the entire world, the entire human race, the last of our brethren and sisters, the last misery and poverty on earth, and God in heaven. Such appeared to me John Paul II.

And to the first group of world servers of this planet he gave the measure and limits of our lives, by comparing us to the stonecutters of a cathedral. In his view we were not likely to see the finished monument of universal peace, of fraternal collaboration and of true harmony between people, but sometimes we would catch a glimpse of it, in a particularly successful achievement, in a problem solved, in the smile of a happy and healthy child, in a conflict avoided, in a reconciliation of minds and hearts achieved. "But know that your work is great and that history will judge your achievements with favour."[1] These words apply to all men and women of good will around this planet who have thrown down the gauntlet for a peaceful, happier and godlier society. Thank you, dear John Paul II, for your blessed visit and for your benediction of the world organization.

[1] United Nations press release, GA/6014 of October 2, 1979.

17

The Reappearance of Christ[1]

You have asked me the question: What does the reappearance of Christ mean in the political, religious and educational fields? To that question I can only answer with a few perceptions, insights and foresights which have grown upon me after working for so many years at the United Nations. It is indeed a place where every day you can see the entire globe, its entire people and the entirety of their dreams, agreements, disagreements, conflicts and evolution. Since everything culminates in this organization and you observe it on a daily basis through the documents you read and the meetings you attend, seeing men and women from various nations trying to find a new path of human destiny, you end up asking yourself: "What does this all mean? Where are we? Is what I am being told the truth? What is happening on this planet? At what moment of evolution or history are we? What is life? What does this complexity mean? What do all our discoveries signify? What do all those divergent views coming from around the globe mean? Is this all vanity? Does it make any sense? Is this a ridiculous planet in the universe? Or on the contrary is what is happening making sense? Does it respond to something? Are we not the partners, the participants, and the instruments of something that goes far beyond us, that was started a long time ago and which will lead to a greater, more beautiful, higher planetary civilization?" These are questions I am asking myself every day. I will give you the answers I have arrived at, especially in the last few years, because I believe that our view is beginning to be clearer.

[1] Transcript of an address to the Arcane School Conference, New York, August 12, 1979.

Things are beginning progressively to fall into a pattern which we had not seen before, because it couldn't be seen, and which foreshadows the world predicted two thousand years ago by someone who had the most luminous insights into the mysteries of life on this planet and in the universe, namely, Christ. This is why, from all I have learned in this global organization, I am more and more drawn to some of the very simple but extremely important teachings of the Christ and of all the great prophets and visionaries. I am increasingly convinced that what they foresaw is beginning to become a reality on this planet and that humanity is transcending or metamorphosing itself into what those great dreamers, visionaries and prophets envisioned. This is what I believe I am living in the glass house on the East River of New York City.

The story, of course, is far from complete: it is only a beginning, the embryo of the world it will be in a few decades, but nevertheless something deep-seated is happening. Things seem to be falling into the following patterns:

At Long Last, a Universal Organization

For the first time ever on this planet, we have a universal organization and global, interdependent thinking. This has never happened before in the political history of this planet. But it is exactly what the great prophets predicted. They always saw the world and humanity as a totality. Today the people sitting in United Nations meetings are forced to see the planet and the human family in their entirety. This is a great new paradigm, an enormous advance in human history, the full significance of which most people do not yet grasp. Only future historians who look back at this last part of our century will be able to understand what really happened on planet Earth.

A Copernican View of Creation

The second element is that the total explosion of knowledge of the human species, which has been so tremendous in the last two hundred years and especially since the end of World War II, has fallen into a prodigiously beautiful pattern. It is a knowledge that goes from the infinitely large to the infinitely small. It is a Copernican view of what the mind has produced, analyzed and pierced in the surrounding reality. I am speaking now only of the mind because the last few centuries were essentially centuries of the supremacy of the mind. It is not necessary to trace the history of why this was so. It was the age of reason, of the mind and of science.

This has produced something incredible: we have been able as a species, as humans, to penetrate far and deep into creation. We have a tremendous knowledge of the universe, of the galaxies, of our solar system. We know the composition of the soils and atmospheres of other planets. We have put man into space; we have satellites turning around this planet. We know our atmosphere, our biosphere, our lithosphere, our hydrosphere, our deserts, our arable land, our mountains, our polar caps, our underground resources of water and minerals. We have penetrated, analyzed, classified and studied everything we could reach from the vastness that surrounds us to infinitely small matter. This is one picture which emerges now in all its splendor. In other words, the human mind has pierced a reality that always existed around us but which we had not penetrated.

We have transcended ourselves with our minds; we have metamorphosed our senses to better understand our planet and the universe in which we live. This is a tremendous advance. And the picture is magnificent. In the end, scientists all tell us that as they reach farther into the universe and find galaxies, spheres of galaxies and innumerable spheres within these galaxies—a world that is ever larger and more incredible—they are still unable to understand the original cause of it all. They are unable to grasp the notion of infinity, and as they go into the infinitely small, you will hear the same answer: that the discovery of further particles and subparticles is endless, that it is an incredible world which fills them with awe for creation. Therefore, scientists and all those who deal with knowledge in the end have only one answer to the mysteries of the universe, namely, that there must be a cause, there must be a reason, there must be a scheme, there must be a universal law. The mathematicians have looked for this law; the biologists have looked for it; the universalists have looked for a universal principle and the theologians have encountered God, the Creator, the alpha and omega of everything. We have now come to the end of the road. The age of reason has been exploited and the result of its discoveries is a magnificent description of the universe, as beautiful as it was seen to be by the prophets. Because they looked into the universe and up to the stars, they always had the concept of the totality of creation.

Our Place in Time

There is another element which is progressively falling into place. It is the concept of time. We see how humanity is forced all of a sudden to extend its time dimension far into the past and far into the future. I have never seen anything like it. When I joined the UN we were not looking far into time. We were just coping with the immediate issues. We have a tendency to forget how recent our knowledge is. It was only in the seventeenth century that Bishop Ussher tried to give a date to our earth. He came to the conclusion that it was born in 4004 B.C.! Then Georges Louis Leclerc, Count de Buffon, in his natural history estimated its age to be five hundred thousand years. Today we have been able to date this planet and its moon at four and a half billion years! You can imagine the prodigious jump humanity has made to date its own home from about six thousand years to four and a half billion years! Astrophysicists further tell us that this planet will be spinning around its sun for another six to eight billion years. This is a new vision which is imposing itself increasingly on the world. It is called, as far as the past is concerned, the preservation of species, of the elements, of nature, of the great monuments and achievements of humankind.

As for the future, it is called the Bimillennium, and is concerned with the economic development of the poor countries, the future of the world climate, of world population, the survival and future of humanity. Year after year one can see the time dimension of our efforts on this planet reach farther into the future. Futurology is a new discipline which was born only since World War II. More and more people are beginning to realize that any correct thinking and behavior on our earth must not only take into account the next twenty or one hundred years but the totality of the time span allotted to this planet. This will cause quite a revolution in thinking and behavior. And again you come to a very simple conclusion: the prophets, Buddha, Christ, all saw it that way. I do not believe there is a single religion on earth that has not conceived our destiny from creation to the apocalypse. Probably one of the most accurate religions in terms of astrophysics is the Hindu religion with its Year of Brahma, a very long period of hundreds of millions of years, marked by creation, preservation, destruction and again creation, preservation and destruction. This is exactly the birth of a star, its preservation through stable hydrogen explosions in the sun, and finally its disintegration again into the universe, where each atom of this present planet and solar system will be reborn in another solar system or star. Thus scientists in the last few years have simply confirmed what the great prophets and outer-space emissaries had proclaimed.

Humanity as an Entity

There is a third element which is becoming increasingly clear. It is the discovery of humanity as an entity. All our history over thousands of years has been the history of groups: tribes, religions, cities, languages, nations. It was always a history based on a group somewhere in the world, a constantly shifting civilization, the story of some major power located in one place on the planet or another. For the first time, in the last thirty years, delegates, scientists, thinkers and servers in the United Nations have discovered that the supreme concern on this planet is humanity itself. This is why, despite all the differences and the fighting for interests, in any United Nations meeting there is, at the end, an adaptation, a greater understanding, because the delegates begin to speak and to act increasingly in the name of humankind. After each successful meeting a sense of happiness radiates from the delegates. It may have been a meeting on human rights, on world population, on natural resources, on human life, be it children, adults, youth or the elderly. The delegates all know that they have participated in global history. This has never existed before on this planet! There have never been any universal meetings like those of the United Nations. Behind the loud words and claims, there is the upsurge of a great tranquil, evolutionary wave towards the protection, survival and fulfillment of the human race on planet Earth. This is now very clear.

Has it occurred to you that the only people who ever took a census of the population of this planet were the Romans? This is why Jesus was born in Bethlehem. Since then no similar censuses were taken until after the Second World War, when the United Nations organized true world censuses. Humanity is now counted and inventoried. We know how many we are. We know our age, our literacy, nutrition, health, levels of development, longevity. All this for the first time has been looked at in its totality, the final objective being to make out of this human family a peaceful, happy entity, in which someday there will be no further need for arms, suspicion, violence and injustices. It is a prodigious story that is unfolding right under our eyes. It is making a little progress each year in some direction. The United Nations is much more than a political organization, it is a paradigm, the expression of a deep, evolutionary change which in the long run will transform the world for the best.

I could also speak of the individual, the uniqueness of each human person, the story of human rights, the individual as a unique cosmos linked with everybody else and with all the elements of this planet. We are unique but we are also interdependent and part of the entirety of creation. That is another truth which was proclaimed by all great religious prophets and which is becoming clear to the international community.

A Holistic View

When you look at the totality, then you see that the picture looks more or less the way all the great religions saw it thousands of years ago, and that year after year the advance, the perception of the human species, through its world organizations is moving more and more towards moral and spiritual relationships. Of late, "economic development" has been replaced by "economic, social, cultural and spiritual development." We find these words in UN reports, in speeches by high UN officials and delegates, in the declarations of human rights. In the World Health Organization a debate on the importance of the soul for the health of the individual has begun. A "holistic approach" is noticeable everywhere. I have never seen anything like it. A completely new dimension is entering the United Nations: holistic medicine, holistic development, concern with the whole human being and with the whole of humanity.

Three hundred years ago Leibniz predicted that humanity would be so thrilled with its scientific discoveries that for centuries it would concentrate on innumerable separate sciences. But he also foresaw that a time would come when humanity would again need to see the totality, the universality, the spiritual dimension of it all. This time seems to have come.

Personally, I was very lucky to be closely associated with the thinking of Dag Hammarskjöld and U Thant. Both of them in different ways were absolutely convinced that the road to happiness and peace went through spirituality. They were emphatic about it in their speeches, writings and conversations. They both attributed to spirituality the highest function in guiding societies on earth. One can begin to see therein the political realization of old visions which were much greater than the one we have today. In the meantime we have made enormous progress on the scientific and material side. We must be grateful for it. Our life span is now much longer than it was at the time of Christ. We know much more than at his time. We therefore cannot condemn the magnificent results of the age of reason and science. But it is now also quite apparent that, after having been successful on the material scene, we must make equal progress in the moral and spiritual spheres.

Concentration on the faculties of intelligence and reason has yielded a golden age of science and progress for humanity. Suppose we concentrated as much energy on the faculties of the heart and the soul? What marvelous benefits we would reap for the further transcendence and fulfillment of the human race: peace, kindness, justice, non-violence, beauty, respect and love for our miraculous planet.

Perhaps such concentration is now indispensable in order to safeguard the benefits yielded by the age of science and intelligence.

Everyone has a different perception of the Christ. I am a Catholic. I have read his sayings many, many times and I have my perception of what the Christ means. In my view He means the following: He is always speaking of the heavenly Father. He always asks us to lift our spirits and to look at the heavens. Secondly, He was the great advocate of love as the ultimate answer to human problems. He also always spoke of peace. "Peace be with you, my peace I leave with you." He further always saw the light. Probably He distinguished himself from all other great visionaries by never accepting duality, the shadows, the dark sides, by being always entirely on the side of light and life: "Follow me and you will see the light." Finally, for me He means belief in resurrection.

Our Father

In my own life and in the world today I can see these messages reappear very potently. For example, it is our knowledge which forces us to look again at the heavens and the stars, to see ourselves as part of the infinite universe and to have endless respect for the Creator, for the Father, as well as a deep thankfulness for the tremendous gift of life and for being able, as distinct from animals, to perceive the greatness of the universe. The prayer, "Our Father," which the Christ has given us himself remains as valid today as ever.

Love

As for love, it is remarkable that both Dag Hammarskjöld and U Thant left us a message of love at the end of their lives. This is extremely important because today our world has become so complex, our knowledge has reached such phenomenal proportions and the interconnections between all the layers of knowledge are such that finally the human person cannot take it any more. As a result, the individual abandons, retreats, withdraws from society or from science, doesn't want to hear anything any more, and is beset by more anxiety than ever before. The words "love" and "faith" combine again into one of those incredible syntheses that the Christ has held before us. We can never understand this earth in its complexity, we can never understand a woman or a man in their complexity; but we can love our planet, love our life, love a person. In the end, given the complexity of the political affairs of this planet, both Dag Hammarskjöld and U Thant came to the conclusion that one could solve them only through love or serene submission to the superiority of creation, in other words, by not wanting to be a master of the planet or of other persons, but by being a servant of that planet and of the people, a servant in time and in space. The more we advance in evolution, the more we will rediscover the tremendous, simplifying, all-encompassing, metascientific virtues of love.

Peace

Peace . . . well, this is the whole United Nations. Peace between nations, peace between groups, peace between races, peace between men and women, peace between generations, peace between all humans, peace with nature. In other words, reciprocal respect and adaptation towards harmonious, happy living. One could say in one sentence that what is happening in the United Nations is a search for a consensus in diversity, a unity that constantly grows while diversity constantly grows too. We are more distinct persons, one from another, than ever before in evolution and this diversification relentlessly continues. It is one of the miracles of evolution on this planet that we move both towards greater unity and cooperation and towards greater diversification and individuality! Again, confronted with such a phenomenon, we find a great simplifying concept left to us by the Christ: peace, or the right, harmonious relations between all groups and all peoples, between humanity and the planet, between peoples and the heavens, between peoples and eternity, while each human being is a unique, unrepeatable child of God and embodiment of the universe.

Light

Light . . . here again I do not know what we would do in the United Nations if we were not constantly on the side of light, of hope, of what is good, what is progress, if we were not constantly believers that it can be done, that we must always throw down our gauntlet for life, for civilization, for the further progress of humanity. This was the Christ one hundred per cent, to the point that He let himself be killed to prove that He would never utilize the methods of darkness, brutality, and evil He condemned on this planet. This is one of the most difficult, most challenging and deepest stories in our history. The largest majority of the people of this planet still believe that it is power, gain, war and coercion that can bring them happiness. We are a minority of people and institutions who believe like Christ that one can never employ the methods one condemns in others, even at the peril of one's own life. This is what is called the miracle of faith, a mystery, a miraculous cement that holds together an individual life as it holds together collective lives. There is nothing we need more in today's world than faith, the belief that goodness and peace can win, the refusal to give up under any circumstance, the molding of every defeat into a victory, of every darkness into light. I wish scientists would study the "miracle of faith." Much of our social future would benefit from their findings. The Hindus call it *prana*, "the vital." It is indeed a vital principle, the energy, the motor of the upward path of human civilization, of our broadening into ever larger discoveries, of our elevation and metamorphosis into an ever greater understanding of the universe and of the divine.

Resurrection

Lastly, there is Christ's message of resurrection. Many people on this planet do not believe in it. But I have lived with a man like U Thant, who constantly held that we were coming from somewhere and that we were going somewhere, that not to believe this made no sense, that whatever he did at any moment of his life would have an impact on the future of humanity to all eternity. He called it the *karma*, or the law whereby no good action is ever lost. Today the biologists tell us that this makes very good sense, because our genes are registering our attitudes, our behavior and our progress, generation after generation. Consequently, our acts and thinking will be transmitted to our descendants. We will be resurrected materially in other life forms on this planet and ultimately into atoms of other stars, but most of all, we will continue to live by the contribution we have made to humanity's improvement through our deeds, thoughts, love and reverence for life during our own incarnations.

Ecumenism

So everywhere I look—and I am not a theologian or a philosopher, I am just a United Nations official trying to make a little sense out of all this—everywhere I see the Christ's luminous messages. They are all still among us, they are coming again to the fore ever more potently. In the present global world they have to express themselves in the ecumenism of religions. The world's major religions in the end all want the same thing, even though they were born in different places and circumstances on this planet. What the world needs today is a convergence of the different religions in the search for and definition of the cosmic or divine laws which ought to regulate our behavior on this planet. World-wide spiritual ecumenism, expressed in new forms of religious cooperation and institutions, would probably be closest to the heart of the resurrected Christ. I would wholeheartedly support the creation of an institutional arrangement in the UN or in UNESCO for a dialogue and cooperation between religions. There is a famous painting and poster which shows Christ knocking at the tall United Nations building, wanting to enter it. I often visualize in my mind another even more accurate painting: that of a United Nations which would be the body of Christ.

I would also like to see published someday a Bible which would show how the United Nations is a modern biblical institution, bent on implementing world-wide the wise precepts and divine commandments of the Bible. I would like to see the same thing done for all great religious or sacred books, such as the Koran, the Grant Sahib, etc.

The ecumenical teachings of the Christ—peace, justice, love, compassion, kindness, human brotherhood, light, faith, rejoicing at life, looking at the heavens and at the Father—must also find their way in world-wide global education. We must give the newcomers into the ceaselessly renewed stream of human life the right education about their planetary home, about their human family, about their past, present and future, about their place in the universe and in time, so that they can flower to their utmost beauty—physically, mentally, morally and spiritually—and become joyful and grateful members of the universe or kingdom of God.

18

Letter to a Canadian Monk

Dear Abbot Veilleux,

I want to comment immediately on the essay you sent me on the role of the monastic subculture in the formation of the monk. You are absolutely right in raising questions which are on the minds of a growing number of people nowadays, namely:

1. How can I cope with the bewildering complexity of knowledge, problems, interdependencies, possibilities, views, aspirations, beliefs, values, dreams and claims to all sorts of rights in this world? Could withdrawal, solitude, faith, meditation and prayer be the answer to my quest for happiness?
2. We know so much about this world and humanity but, like Faust, we are not wiser than before. May the answer be in mysticism, love for God, poetry, escape of the individual from the earth to the divine?
3. In the West, we have food, shelter, health, hygiene, security and education and yet we do not seem to be much happier than before. Why is that? How, when and where can we find happiness?
4. What is the purpose of life? Why am I here? Was there anything before me and will there be anything after me? Who am I? How do I relate to the rest of the world, to the people, to the heavens and to eternity?
5. How can there be peace, goodness and happiness on this planet? How can the sins of institutions, particularly of nations, be coped with? How can they continue seeking endless power instead of serving the people and humanity?

In your efforts at total rethinking, it would be good to establish this *problématique* of our time, taking into account the profound historical dichotomy which exists between the developed and the developing countries. In the latter, survival at birth, food, a decent life, education, hygiene and longer lives are the priorities. This is why materialism has a much greater justification in these countries. One might even say that materialism is the first spirituality. First one has to live.

You should ignore totally all earlier thinkers, including Plato, Hegel, Kant, Marx, Nietzsche, etc. We live in a completely different world and time. If they were alive today, they would be the first to discard their theories and offer new ones more appropriate for our era. They would probably say that care for our planetary home and for the survival and happiness of the human race are the predominant problems of our time. Ours is a period of a magnitude and of potential human development of which they did not have the faintest idea.

Facing this *problématique*, you have the eternal monastic or "self-apartheid" solution as one of the multiple possible answers. The question is: what can monks offer the individual of our time, what can they offer the world, what can they offer powerful institutions?

And the answers can be quite simple: in the monasteries of the world, all humanity is already united with itself and with the heavens. Or to say with young Pachomius: "To serve humanity all the days of my life, that is my wish."

Humans always need ideals to live by. Lost as we believe we are among the four and a half billion people of this planet, we need exceptional beings who give us a luminous vision, elevate us, make us feel better and help us understand how great a miracle human life really is in the universe. It is strange that solitude in a prison or in a monastery should often produce a mystical elevation and a deep spiritual experience. Perhaps prison, monasticism and the image of death are among the most powerful means to make us realize the true priorities and value of life. Some people also—and it is usually a mark of greatness—are able to touch the innermost fibers of life right amidst the action and turmoils of the world. Dag Hammarskjöld, for example, was a great mystic in action. All his work was performed in accord with this belief: "In our era, the road to holiness necessarily passes through the world of action." For him, world service was an overflow of love, of personal transcendence into the realm of feeling for the world and for its people. He would have agreed fully with Pachomius' exclamation. Mysticism, religion and the awareness of death are close cousins of art and poetry: they are all manifestations of a deep love and endless astonishment for the mystery of life. The mystic, the religious person, the monk, the poet and the artist, by expanding their hearts and souls into total reality, are able to perceive the material and immaterial universe in a way which will forever remain forbidden to the mind. Love might well be in the end the highest perception within the reach of human beings.

You are indeed great experts in many fields where basic rethinking has begun on this planet: inner life, frugal life, simple life, manual work, tilling the land, handicrafts, solitude, study, meditation, prayer and communion with God. Hence the immense success of a Thomas Merton with the youth of today. He had assimilated all you had to offer and gave it back with an overflowing heart, as a master, as a lived personal experience and with the accents of truth without which no one believes anyone any more these days. In view of the energy crisis, the food crisis, inflation, etc., monastic experiences could be subjects of much scientific curiosity and inquiry, as the Amish ways of life have recently been. You have something important to offer the world and you should be studied as possible answers to the problems of our time by psychologists, sociologists, economists, etc.

This applies to all religions. They have ancient answers which modern man has all too often forgotten. But religions are *dans le monde* (in the world), whereas monasteries are apart from the world. They keep intact in their purity the old, instinctive answers to the mysteries and fears of life, developed by those who in all cultures consider it their vocation to pray and meditate for the entire group. You can play today the same role you have played so often before when the world passed through periods of confusion and anxiety. But there is not much time to lose. You must go to the heart of the matter and do what all great monastic leaders did over the ages: write down a set of monastic rules for our time and possibly conceive two world monastic orders, one composed of all the monastic groups around the world living apart from the world; and another, new order of world servers deeply immersed in the outside world—politics, public service, business, education, art, etc. Those would spend temporary periods in monasteries to refresh and purify themselves in solitude, contemplation, sunrises and sunsets, nature, communion with God, the universe and eternity, the practice of peace, serenity, service to others, frugality, poverty, humility and love, all those great virtues which are your specialty. Create such an order and I will join it forthwith, stimulated by the good example of U Thant, the Buddhist who in the middle of the world's turmoil never ceased to be a monk.

Speaking of U Thant, I have observed that his beloved classification of human needs and virtues is also the main foundation of all monastic orders: physical life (respect for one's body, manual work), mental life (learning, extended being through knowledge and understanding), moral life (practice of brotherhood, compassion, kindness and love), and spiritual life (communion with God, eternity and the universe, mystical comprehension of the cosmos). He showed us by his example how one's life can be beautifully geared to these four basic needs and qualities of humanity.

Like everything else, renewal consists in restating old eternal truths in a modern context, which today means a world-wide, universal, planetary context encompassing our enormous knowledge and extensive experience with living. You must write down the universal rules of monasticism, the essence of all that is true and meaningful to you, for you are among the truest and most advanced seekers of the truth. At the same time, the many diverse existing monastic traditions can continue to flourish in their rich diversity like the flowers of a garden. Unity in diversity is one of the basic laws of the universe, as it is the law for a garden.

In doing so, do not consult anyone but yourself and God. Do not hold meetings or ugly think-tanks. Someone has to sit down and give the first great outline. It is with reformers and visionaries as it is with all great masters: you have to do it all yourself. No one will help you, no one can do it for you, if only because the task seems insuperable. Hence, helpers tend to lose themselves in secondary, confusing, dilatory thinking and exercises. Once you have produced the first fruit which is ripe in you, then you can send it to a few friends for comments and advice. I would be very happy to be counted among those and to become one of the first members of a new world monastic order.

The path opened by Merton and by the Eastern sages must now be crowned in modern terms: with rules, structures, institutions, codes and the offering of a philosophy of divine fulfillment on earth.

We need a world organization in which all the world's monastic movements can cooperate, learn from each other, live with each other and define humanity's divine spiritual laws hidden in our hearts and in the cosmos.

Humanity is ready for a new culture. That culture must include the benefits derived from solitude, meditation, prayer and spirituality right in the middle of daily action and life. Dag Hammarskjöld and U Thant were two living examples of such modern monks, one a mystic in his own right, the other a humble Buddhist applying his faith honestly and painstakingly. There is no reason why our planet should not be a floating cathedral in the universe, a vast temple to God or a monastery. What better fate could we plan for? What a sight it would be for extraterrestrial visitors to see us as a planet of praying, grateful, heavenly beings, fully aware of the miraculous consciousness bestowed upon us in the vast universe. *Oui, le monachisme pourrait considérer le monde comme un immense monastère.* Yes, monasticism could consider the world as a vast monastery! In our era the road to sanctity passes indeed through the worlds of both action and solitude.

I hope these few thoughts from an international civil servant might be of some use to you.

May peace, love and happiness always be yours.

19

Global Spirituality, the Need for Faith and What Sisters Can Do[1]

Many sisters would be interested in your ideas about global spirituality, especially since there is such an emphasis on evangelization these days. How did you discover a global spirituality?

I have been working in the United Nations for more than thirty years. During all these years, I saw that the problems brought to the world organization were primarily related to the physical well-being of peoples, such as the prevention of wars, hunger, sickness, epidemics, natural disasters, handicaps, etc. Then there were problems relating to the intellectual aspects of life, especially education and literacy, which enable people to have more dignified, fulfilled lives. In addition, the United Nations was getting increasingly involved with ethical and moral problems, like codes of human rights, codes of conduct for transnational corporations, the treatment of prisoners by the police, of patients by scientists and doctors, etc. If you read the Charter of the United Nations you will find it to be an ethical code, a sort of Ten Commandments for nations. However, one day someone asked me the question: "Isn't there also a spiritual dimension to the United Nations?"

At that time, I came across the views of two of our Secretaries-General, namely Dag Hammarskjöld and U Thant. They had both concluded that the physical, material, mental and moral problems of humanity could only be solved satisfactorily if we had a spiritual view

[1] A Message of Hope from an Optimist at the United Nations, interview with Sister Mary Madden, C.S.J. published in the magazine *Sisters Today*, October 1979.

of world affairs. Of course, the question arose immediately: how can one speak of a global spirituality in a world of so many religions and atheists, besides there being religions like Buddhism, Jainism and Sikhism which have no God? However, there is a common denominator when humans see themselves as part of a very mysterious and beautiful universe. From that awe emerges a spiritual approach to life. Everything becomes sacred, understandable and miraculous. How can one kill or harm anyone who is sacred? This will be the new common path or story of humanity as the human race matures and sees its stupendous place and luck in creation. Every religion tells this story in a different way, but all offer us explanations which no scientist has been able to give us regarding the mysterious force which rules the universe.

When we relate to this force, to God, everything falls into place. As long as humanity does not do this, no true, lasting answers will be found for our earthly problems. I often try to imagine what would happen if the delegates to the UN General Assembly in addition to opening each session with a minute of prayer or silence, put this question to God: "Look, dear God, here we are. We have all these problems. We are rather lost. Help us, enlighten us to see all this more clearly." I am sure the problems of the world would become much simpler to resolve if we related to someone who is above and beyond us. I hope that someday the United Nations will prepare a yearly report to God.

All religions see humankind's place in total time, from creation to the apocalypse. The soul is not merely here for a short number of solar years. We come from somewhere and we are going somewhere, as part of the great stream of the universe. If we do not see this in our lives, we cannot find happiness and serenity and adopt a right moral stand. Even biologists tell us that our behavior is recorded in genes. Scientists are convinced that the long-term view of life is the only correct way of visualizing the ascent of the human species.

So this is how I came to a global spirituality. I believe that the religions have many of the answers which the political world is seeking, because they have been here many more years than the United Nations. We should consult them. Dag Hammarskjöld and U Thant were absolutely right when they considered that world affairs needed to be inspired, guided, elevated and ruled by a global spirituality, and that political leaders needed similarly to be guided by a personal spirituality.

You are called the "optimist in residence" at the United Nations. Have you seen any miracles happening lately?

My optimism does not mean so much that I believe in miracles. The miracle is that the belief of people that something can be done produces the desired result. Optimism and pessimism both have their nutrients. As Norman Cousins has written: "Pessimism and optimism are significantly more than opposite moods. Just as despair sets the stage for its own omens, so reasoned hope provides the essential nutrients for a flowering of the spirit that enhances life, thereby contributing regenerative energies to the shared living environment." It is as with prayer, which visualizes what we deeply desire and helps it to materialize. I believe that if one feels that something is possible it becomes possible. If you feel it is impossible it becomes impossible, or its chances of becoming possible are substantially reduced. This is very important. The religions call it the mystery of faith, because it is very difficult to explain, and the miracle of faith, because it produces miracles. From the moment one has a particular faith, that faith materializes. This is true for all walks of life. If one has a tendency to feel sick, one is very likely to become sick. If one feels marvelously happy and in good health, automatically one's trillions of little cells feel it: they are anxiously awaiting this central message, guidance and encouragement to well-being. One must orchestrate with great care and optimism one's cosmos, or else the little cells find it difficult to work together in harmony, i.e., in health. Similarly, it is very important to be hopeful and optimistic in a place like the United Nations where one faces every conceivable problem and trouble in the world. As a matter of fact the United Nations is a kind of clinic for world accidents and therapy. At the UN more than anywhere else one must feel like a doctor and have reasonable hope; even if we do not succeed today, we will tomorrow. Someday even armaments will disappear from this planet. One has to keep after what one considers the truth all the time and relentlessly. I am sure that we will have peace on this planet, if we constantly believe in it. More and more people are working towards it all around the globe. Their efforts will not remain forever without effect.

Many hopes I have had with regard to the United Nations have materialized. I dreamed that it would become someday universal. It is universal today, the first world-wide organization ever on this planet. A few years ago I proposed a world conference on science and technology to Dag Hammarskjöld. I asked the question: "Why do we not apply our intelligence to the tropical and equatorial areas as we do to the northern countries?" I come from a steel and coal region in Lorraine; I often wondered whether, if coal and iron had not been located in the same place, we would have invented steel. Why don't we look at the rest of the world to see if miracles like this are not possible elsewhere? Well, we had two world conferences on that subject. Similarly, I had hoped that world concern would develop for our planet's four hundred fifty million handicapped. It took some doing, but in 1981 we finally had an International Year of Disabled Persons. A few years ago, with a few colleagues, we thought that we needed a world conference on water because what was happening with energy would also happen to our water supply. The first reaction of governments was: "Why should we have another world conference?" Well, we had it! And in the meantime water indeed became a problem of growing concern to many countries. We have also been preaching that we must prepare for the arrival of hundreds of millions of old people on this planet. Longevity is increasing. People in developing countries are also getting older. In the next twenty years there will be hundreds of millions of newly old people creating problems we have never encountered on this planet. Well, a world assembly on aging is being held in 1982. I have thus seen a good many dreams for humanity materialize. As a matter of fact there were so many of them that I have gained an unprecedented faith in the future of humanity, and hence have been called the "optimist in residence at the UN," a title of which I am rather proud. But miracles are not handed to one. One has to work for them. They are the fruit of one's faith, hope and optimism, which help nurture them and bring them forth to life and love.

At this stage of my life, after so many years of observation of the world scene, I have come to the conclusion that our planet, all life on it and in particular human life, is a manifestation of cosmic or divine forces of the universe. Within us therefore resides a basic cosmic force that impels us to respond to our evolutionary duties and to be in favor of life and of our further ascent. If we don't, we are abandoned by this central, all-pervading force and we die individually or collectively. Faith in life and in our future is therefore the most vital force we must rely on to continue successfully on our strange, unfathomable journey in the universe. This is what the

Christ and many other messengers from the outer heavens have told us: believe in life, in light, in resurrection, in the accomplishment of the will of God or the cosmos. This applies to me and to you as individuals as it applies to the entire world society.

As an international diplomat and Catholic layman, how do you see the role of sisters today in the new trend of world concerns?

Sisters can play a tremendously important role for two reasons. The first is that we have arrived at a stage of evolution when women will play a much more important role than ever before. It is not a question of equality of men and women. It goes much deeper. What is happening is that the first two or more million years of our evolution on this planet were of an aggressive nature. People had to fight for their food, for their survival, for their existence. For two million years aggression and fighting were the dominant features of this planet. Even today, groups fight for their "security" and preponderance. We have come to the point where this has reached its limits. We are now entering a period when the aggressiveness of men will give way to the values of women. Men have been the masters also of the last two or three hundred years because it was the so-called age of reason. Sentiment was pushed aside almost completely. Everything had to be done through "intelligence." That intelligence has enabled us to make fantastic discoveries, but now limitations have set in.

Reason suddenly is unable to give us the answers to the complexities of creation. This is why, at this juncture, we need to turn to other values which women possess instinctively and naturally, i.e., in a most advanced form. A woman who has a child is not reasoning with herself about the relations with the child. It is all expressed very simply and beautifully in the word "love." It is a relationship which one cannot define, which goes totally beyond reason. Since women nurture the family and the child, this is her specialty. What we need today on this planet is more love than reason. We must now fashion a moral world based on the great virtues of truth, love, compassion and beauty. The woman specializes in these virtues. Beauty is very important to her. It is the world of the woman to make her home beautiful, to make herself beautiful and to make the lives of others beautiful. And when it comes to love, it is increasingly apparent that the main challenge of our age is to love the entire creation, to love our planet, to love the human family, to love each other and to love the mysterious Creator in heaven. We have entered the great loving process of humanity. And we find again the woman as the experienced specialist, in the avant-garde of evolution.

As for sisters, they are not only women but altruistic women. They have decided to devote their lives to the service of others. Many sisters, therefore, are involved in education, taking care of the handicapped, of the elderly, of the poor, rejected and lonely. They are present at the moment of death. When my grandfather died there was a sister at his side helping him to die. There are not many people who will help you to die. Sister Teresa is the epitome of sisterhood when she exclaims:

"The poor are brothers and sisters in the same family, created by the same loving God. If you do not know them, you do not love them, and you do not serve them. We must love until it hurts."

Sisters are great specialists in suffering. We need them very much today. The sisters can be very helpful with their experience and concern for social, humanitarian issues such as those of the International Year of the Child, UNICEF, the International Year of Disabled Persons, the Refugees, the Hunger campaigns, the World Assembly on Aging. I have proposed to the Catholic authorities that they should not wait for some of these conferences to take place, but should prepare a long time ahead and gather the experience of the Church all around the world. In this way they would be able to advise the United Nations how to deal with these problems—for example, that of the elderly—because they know so much more than we. The Vatican should ask the sisters to share their wisdom and experience learned from their direct service to the poor and elderly.

Most of all, we should not forget their greatest contribution of all, that is, the spiritual dimension of the sisters' service in prayer and contemplation. Our world has a very great need for deeper spirituality. We need the sisters who are completely devoted to contemplation. They could play a very great role by praying for the peace and goodness of the world, especially for those who are involved in action for peace, like myself and all United Nations servers. What we need most in the United Nations is prayer for our success. It is faith-filled prayer that moves the mountains of misunderstanding and prejudice. I have suggested to the Vatican that there ought to be a campaign of prayer for the United Nations. The Church pays more attention to the problem of peace and not enough attention to the people and institutions already involved in bringing about peace on this planet. I could count on my fingers the rare number of times I have heard church prayers for the United Nations. And yet we need to know that you are praying for us. This will give us the strength we require to believe that peace can become a reality on our planet.

The United Nations also needs prayers because it is not infallible. Under pressure of political events, the United Nations sometimes takes a stand with which the churches do not agree. The churches may be right and not the United Nations. For example, there is the issue of population. The United Nations has adopted a world plan for action on population and the only voice against this plan was that of the Holy See. Against one hundred and fifty nations, the Holy See raised its voice in favor of life. It is true that we have a fantastic population explosion. It is true that it is no good for a woman to have seven or eight children and see them die around her because she is not able to feed them. However, we should not fall into the opposite error and suddenly rejoice at stopping life. If we could save the five hundred and fifty billion dollars spent each year on armaments, we could accommodate many more people at the banquet table of life.

The Church is right to keep an eye on issues because sometimes new ethical values coming out of the United Nations are not correct and are tinged with national, short-term interests. The Holy See has promised to support the United Nations when it is on the right road. If it is not, the Holy See, which is represented at the United Nations, will tell us. So far, the Holy See has never hesitated to tell the United Nations when it is wrong. We need the wisdom of the ages which belongs to the Church. We need most of all her prayers. Please tell the sisters to pray for us.

20

Spiritual Education: A World of Difference

The 1981 United States Convention of Catholic Educators and Librarians asked me for my views on the theme: "Catholic Education, A World of Difference." The statement I made could be equally valid for any denomination of the Christian faith, and it could be rewritten and adapted to every major faith of this planet. What lessons we would derive from such an exercise! What progress we would make towards a global spiritual understanding and teaching of our prodigious journey in the vast, mysterious universe!

Not being an educator, I have thought a lot of how I could make a useful contribution to your convention. I have come to the conclusion that I might tell you how I would educate the children of this world on the basis of my thirty-three years of experience at the United Nations and as a Catholic Christian. I will offer you a world core curriculum aimed at all grades, levels and forms of education, including adult education.

The starting point is that every hour 6,000 of our brothers and sisters die and 15,000 children are born on this planet. The newcomers must be educated so that they can benefit from the acquired knowledge, skills and art of living of humanity, enjoy happy and fulfilled lives, and contribute in turn to the continuance, maintenance and further ascent of humanity on a well-preserved planet.

Alas, many newly born will never reach school age. One out of ten will die before reaching the age of one and another four per cent will die before the age of five.

There is a second prior problem: we must try by every possible means to prevent children from reaching school age with handicaps.

It is estimated that ten per cent of all the world's children have a handicap of a physical, sensory or mental nature by the time they reach school age. In the developing countries, an unforgivable major cause is still malnutrition. I am glad to note that your convention has a special workshop on education of the handicapped. This is most timely, since the United Nations has proclaimed 1981 as International Year of Disabled Persons (IYDP) to draw the world's attention to its 450 million disabled people.

Thirdly, my ideal curriculum presupposes that there are schools for all the children of the world. Alas, this is not the case. There are still 814 million illiterates on this planet. Humanity has done wonders in educating its people: we have reduced the percentage of illiterates of the world adult population from 32.4 per cent to 28.9 per cent between 1970 and 1980, a period of phenomenal population growth. But between now and the year 2000, 1.6 billion more people will be added to this planet and we are likely to reach a total of 6.1 billion people in that year. Ninety per cent of the increase will be in the developing countries where the problem of education is most severe. As a result, the total number of illiterates could climb to 950 million by the Bimillennium.

Education for all remains, therefore, a first priority on this planet, as every Catholic missionary can tell you. This is why UNESCO has rightly adopted a World Literacy plan for the year 2000.

With all these miseries and limitations still with us, it remains important, nevertheless, to lift one's sight and to begin thinking of a world core curriculum since Catholicism, as the name indicates, is universal. The great merit of being a Catholic is to be more than a member of a nation, of a race, of a culture, of a language, of a profession. It is to be a member of the entire human family, a member of a heavenly, universal family ruled by divine precepts. Catholic education is therefore far ahead of purely earthbound, civilian education lacking a spiritual, universal dimension. This is true of all affairs of this world. After my many years of world service, I can say unequivocally that only a spiritual approach or divine consciousness will permit us to solve our earthly problems. This is what all great religious prophets, visionaries and heavenly emissaries have told us for thousands of years. This is the true meaning of ecumenism as proclaimed by Vatican II and I would hope that educators of all the major religions would put their heads together and show a confused and not very happy world the tremendous benefits to be derived from a global, spiritual education.

Several decades will still pass before nations admit the necessity of a curriculum which would encompass all national educational systems. But it will come. The new global circumstances and concerns of our planet make it imperative that we begin considering it. Today's planetary sciences and technology will unify the world in the same way as road and bridge building made the Roman Empire and railroads unified the United States as well as Russia. The challenge to Catholic education is therefore to integrate fully the advanced results of our scientific, technological and social knowledge into its universal, spiritual vision of human life and destiny in the universe and in time.

My curriculum aims at providing a simple synthesis of all the complex knowledge acquired in the last few centuries, especially during the last three decades. One of the main objectives of education is to put sense and order into things and to give the children a correct view of the planet and of the circumstances in which they will live. I outlined the need for a new educational approach a few years ago in an essay, "The Need for Global Education," which has played a part in inducing several governments, including that of the United States, to give consideration to a new type of world education.

As I do in the United Nations, where all human knowledge, concerns, efforts and aspirations converge, I would organize the fundamental lifelong objectives of education around four categories:

  I. Our planetary home and place in the universe
 II. The human family
III. Our place in time
IV. The miracle of individual human life

I. Our Planetary Home and Place in the Universe

The first major segment of the curriculum should deal with our prodigious knowledge of planet Earth. Humanity has been able, of late, to produce a magnificent picture of our planet and of its place in the universe.

From the infinitely large to the infinitely small, everything fits today into a very simple and clear pattern. The list of subjects in this first segment should be as follows, as we use it in the United Nations:

The infinitely large: the universe, the stars and outer space
Our relations with the sun
The earth's physics
The earth's climate
The atmosphere
The biosphere
The seas and oceans
The polar caps
The earth's land masses
The earth's arable lands
The deserts
The mountains
The earth's water
Plant life
Animal life
Human life
The earth's energy
The earth's crust and depths
The earth's minerals
The infinitely small: microbiology, genetics, chemistry and nuclear physics

At each of these levels humanity has made incredible progress and knows an enormous amount. Astrophysicists tell us how stars and planets are born and die. We know the physics, atmospheres and even soils of other planets. Thanks to man-made satellites, we have a total view of our globe, of our atmosphere, of our seas and oceans and land masses. We know our complicated climate through a new science called climatology. We know our polar caps. For the first time ever, we possess a soil and land map for the entire planet. We know our mountains. We know our total water resources. We know our deserts. We know our flora and fauna. We know part of the crust of our earth. Our knowledge reaches far down into the microbial, genetic and cellular worlds, into the realm of the atom and its particles and subparticles. We have an incredible, beautiful, vast picture of our place in the universe. If a teacher wishes to give children a glimpse of the tremendous expanse of our knowledge, all he or she has to do is to have them visit on the same day an astronomical observatory and an atomic bubble chamber!

All this knowledge culminates in the United Nations or in one of its specialized agencies or world conferences. For each of the above items, I could give vivid examples of intensive world cooperation: e.g., on astrophysics and outer space, the UN has convened two world conferences; on the climate, the World Meteorological Organization has a Global Atmospheric Research Program and convened in 1979 a first World Climate Conference; on air space and aviation, we have the International Civil Aviation Organization; on the seas and oceans, there is the UN's Conference on the Law of the Sea; the ozonosphere and the entire biosphere are of concern to the UN Environment Program. I could go on and on, down to world cooperation in genetics and microbiology in UNESCO and in the World Health Organization, and in nuclear physics in the International Atomic Energy Agency. As a matter of fact, it is absolutely essential and in our enlightened self-interest to teach the children about this international cooperation so that they can see that humanity is beginning to work together and that there is good hope for a better world. There is a dire need for a good textbook on the UN and on international cooperation for Catholic schools.

The above framework allows us to present our planetary and universal knowledge to all people and particularly to children in a simple, beautiful manner. Humanity has discovered and pierced piecemeal the reality that surrounds us, and now this knowledge falls into a magnificent total pattern which must be taught to humans from childhood on. They wish to be told about their correct place in the universe. The Greeks' and Pascal's genial view of the infinitely large and the infinitely small has been filled in by science and provides the framework for much of today's international cooperation and daily lives of peoples. We can now give children a breath-taking view of the beauty and teeming, endless richness of creation as has never been possible before in human evolution. It should make them glad to be alive and to be human. It should also prepare them with excitement for a vast number of professions and make them better and more responsible members of the human race, henceforth the caretaker of our planet.

What special contributions can a Catholic Christian or spiritual education add to these "civilian" results, which are mostly the products of the scientific and rational age by which the world has now been ruled for several centuries? There are many of them, but let me mention four principal ones:

First, the scientists have now come to the end of their wisdom. Humans are simply incapable of grasping the vastness of creation and all its mysteries. We cannot understand the notions of the infinitely large, of the infinitely small and of eternity. Even the notions of matter and energy, of objectivity and subjectivity are being challenged today. Beyond the elation at our discoveries, there is a certain despair at our incapacity to comprehend the totality. This is where spirituality or religion comes in. Science in my view is part of the spiritual process; it is a transcendence and elevation of the human race into an ever vaster knowledge and consciousness of the universe and of its unfathomable, divine character.

Secondly, our wonder at the magnificence of creation is today greater than ever. What a beautiful picture of the universe we can present to our children! We should describe it with at least as much love, poetry, exaltation and ecstasy as did the writers of the Bible. Teachers have a wonderful story to tell, stories of endless miracles from a galaxy to the genetic factory contained in a cell, from the courses of the planets to the life of a flower and the whirling of electrons in an atom. Spiritual and religious awe, endless respect for the magnificence of the universe and for the greatness of the Creator will ensue.

Thirdly, we can elicit pride at being humans, at being able, above all species, to go so far in the comprehension of the universe. We can show children and people that there is something divine, miraculous and tremendous in being human, that God must have a special design for us, that our evolution makes more and more sense, that it will continue at ever higher levels until this planet has finally become a showcase in the universe, a planet of God. This will give children a sense of participation in the building of the earth, of becoming artisans of the will of God and thus co-creators with Him.

Fourthly, as vividly described in the story of the Tree of Knowledge, having decided to become like God through knowledge and our attempt to understand the heavens and the earth, we have also become masters in deciding between good and bad: every invention of ours can be used for good and bad all along the above Copernican tapestry of our knowledge: outer-space technology can be used for peace or for killer satellites, aviation for transportation or for dropping bombs, the atom for energy or for nuclear destruction, etc.

This gives Catholic, Christian and all spiritual educators a marvelous opportunity to teach a new morality and ethics all along the scale and thus to prepare responsible citizens, workers, scientists, geneticists, physicists and scores of other professionals, including a new badly needed category: world managers and caretakers.

II. *The Human Family*

There is a second segment on which humanity has also made tremendous progress of late: not only have we taken cognizance of our planet and of our place in the universe, but we have also taken stock of ourselves! This is of momentous importance, for henceforth our story in the universe is basically that of ourselves and of our planet. For a proper unfolding of that story, we had to know its two main elements well: the planet and ourselves. This has been accomplished since World War II. The planetary and human inventories are practically complete.

When the UN was founded no one knew what the world population was. A UN Population Commission was created, sample surveys were conducted and agreements reached on the world-wide collection of population statistics and the holding of world censuses. We thus learned in 1951 that we were two and a half billion people. Today we are four and a half billion! A population explosion which could have gone unnoticed was detected. The necessary global warnings were given and humanity is now responding with slower birth rates to the lowering of death rates.

We have learned so much about humanity since the end of World War II: we now know how many we are; where we live; how long we live; how many males, females, youths and elderly there are. This knowledge is being constantly improved and refined. We have a quantitative knowledge of our human family which we never had before at any time in history. We know ourselves also qualitatively: our levels of living, of nutrition, of health, of literacy, of employment, etc. We also have records of our progress: we know how many literates are being added to this planet each year; we know that by eradicating smallpox the number of the blind in the world was reduced by half, etc. Incidentally, it was no small achievement to have accommodated 2 billion more people on this planet within a short period of thirty years!

The human family has looked at itself in a series of major conferences on population, human settlements, women, youth, races, economic development, etc. After the International Year of the Child, we had the International Year of Disabled Persons, and in 1982 we will hold a World Assembly on Aging. As a result of so many efforts, we have an unprecedented inventory and knowledge of humanity. That fundamental, up-to-date knowledge must be conveyed to all the children of the world.

There is a further major aspect of the human family on which we have made substantial progress during the last decades, namely, our society and its man-made groupings. We are indeed a species that likes to congregate and subdivide itself into any conceivable group based on physical, geographic, qualitative or ideological aspects: races, sexes, age groups, nations, provinces, cities, rich and poor, religions, languages, social systems, forms of government, corporations, professions, institutions, associations, etc. Many of these are inherited from the past: thus we enter the global age with more than 150 nations, 5,000 languages, scores of religions, etc. Other entities are new, such as world organizations, multinational corporations and transnational associations.

All these groups are being studied and heard in the United Nations and its agencies. What this all means is as yet little understood. Formation of entities or the social biology of the human species, from the world society to the individual, is still a rather primitive science.

The first task of the United Nations is to build bridges, peace and harmony between these groups, to listen to their views and perceptions, to prevent them from blowing each other up and endangering the entire planet, to seek what each group has to contribute, to understand their legitimate concerns, values, denominators and objectives, and to grasp the meaning of the vast and complex functioning of life from the largest to the most minute, from the total society to the individual, from human unity to an endless, more refined diversity.

It is a vast, unprecedented, mind-boggling challenge but it would help if our second great segment of the world core curriculum were organized as follows:

The Human Family

QUANTITATIVE CHARACTERISTICS

The total world population and its changes
Human geography and migrations

Human longevity
Races
Sexes
Children
Youth
Adults
The elderly
The handicapped

QUALITATIVE CHARACTERISTICS

Our levels of nutrition
Our levels of health
Our standards of life (rich and poor)
Our skills and employment
Our levels of education
Our moral levels
Our spiritual levels

HUMAN GROUPINGS

The family
Human settlements
Professions
Corporations
Institutions
Nations
Regions
Religions
Multinational business
Transnational networks
World organizations

What will be important in such a curriculum is the dynamic aspect of the relations between humanity and our planet: we now have good inventories; we know the elements of the great evolutionary problems confronting us, but we barely stand at the beginning of the planetary management phase of human history: demographic options, resources management, environmental protection, conflict resolution, the management of peace, justice and progress for all, the optimization of human life in space and in time. The

United Nations and its specialized agencies offer the first examples of attempts at global management in all these fields and must therefore occupy a prominent and necessary place in the world's curricula. The earlier we do this, the better it will be for our survival and fulfillment.

Again, what an immense contribution Catholic and Christian education can bring to a better understanding and teaching of the human family and its components: a proper population policy which respects the right to life; the equality of races; Christ's teachings and the Church's long experience with children, youth, the family, adults, the elderly; the equality of sexes, peace, justice, reverence for life; help to the poor, the downtrodden and the handicapped. The social experience of the Church vastly surpasses that of the young United Nations and its agencies. This is why the Holy See has become so close to the United Nations, offering its vision, help and experience in the solution of most difficult world problems. When I read documents emanating from the Holy See dealing with social issues, I sometimes have the impression that I am reading United Nations documents. What marvelous opportunities the UN, its agencies and its world conferences offer Catholics to participate in the making of a better world! The Holy See has fully understood it and maintains important missions at the seats of all the UN agencies. His Holiness is always ready to help the United Nations in its endeavors, the last example being his appeal for the world's handicapped on January 1, 1981, the opening day of the IYDP.

More importantly, all the teachings of Catholicism and Christianity derive from a spiritual, divine or cosmic understanding of the unity of the human race under God, of the sanctity of life and the consequent abhorrence and condemnation of war, violence, terrorism, armaments, injustices, poverty, discrimination, hatred and untruthfulness. Popes Paul VI and John Paul II in their historical visits to the United Nations and their yearly messages on the Day of Peace have articulated a full doctrine of peace and right human relations for our planet. These texts should be used in the teaching of this vital segment of the world curriculum. They go far beyond the rational and "interest" language of the political world and add a much-needed spiritual, altruistic dimension to human efforts. They dare to speak of love for our planet, for the heavens and for all our brothers and sisters, a word very little used in the contemporary political world. What beautiful teachings can unfold in Catholic schools around these concepts: concern for the environment as an act of love for our planet; concern for the poor as an act of love for all our human brothers and sisters; turning to God as a guide for our behavior, etc. What a deep truth and tremendous vision Christ has given us! No wonder He has survived all political regimes and ideologies, and He offers us today as correct universal answers to humanity's problems as ever. As a matter of fact, this is the great hour for a spiritual world renaissance. The supreme reality of the human family, universal and interdependent, as seen by Christ and by all great religious leaders must now become the world's major political objective. The time has come for the implementation of a spiritual vision of world affairs. The entire planet must elevate itself again into the spiritual, cosmic throbbing of the universe.

III. Our Place in Time

In the same way as humanity is taking cognizance of its correct place in the universe, it is now also forced to look at its correct place in time or eternity.

When I joined the United Nations in 1948 there was very little time perspective. The word "futurology" did not even exist. Some nations who had five-year economic plans were derided, because it was believed that no one on this planet could plan for five years ahead! How the world has changed since then! Today every nation is planning for at least twenty years ahead. At the world level, the UN has adopted a world economic development strategy for the 1980s; the Food and Agriculture Organization has a World Food Plan 2000, the World Health Organization a World Health Plan 2000, UNESCO a World Literacy Plan 2000; UN demographers provide us with population projections for the next hundred years and the World Meteorological Organization tries to forecast our climate for the next several hundred years.

Something similar is happening with regard to the past. Today we know that our planet is more than 4.5 billion years old and we have developed a vast knowledge of our paleontological and archaeological past. Astrophysicists tell us that our sun—a star of stabilized light hydrogen explosions—will remain in existence for another 6 to 8 billion years before we vanish again into the universe to become other stars and planets.

Thus humanity is forced to expand its time dimension tremendously into the past and into the future: we must preserve the natural elements inherited from the past and necessary for our life and survival (air, water, soils, energy, animals, fauna, flora, genetic materials). We also want to preserve our cultural heritage, the landmarks of our own evolution and history, in order to see the unfolding and magnitude of our cosmic journey. At the same time we must think and plan far ahead into the future in order to hand over to succeeding generations a well-preserved and better-managed planet. What does this mean for a world curriculum? It means that we must add a time dimension to the above layers, each of which has a past, a present and a future:

The universe:	past,	present,	future
Our sun	"	"	"
Our globe	"	"	"
Our climate	"	"	"
Our biosphere	"	"	"

etc. down to the cell, genes and the atom

The human family:	past,	present,	future
Our age composition	"	"	"
Our levels of health	"	"	"
Our standards of living	"	"	"
Nations	"	"	"
Religions	"	"	"
World organizations	"	"	"

etc. down to the individual

Taken together, our present knowledge and responsibilities on our miraculous little planet are of awesome complexity and magnitude. It will take great vision and honesty to achieve the harmony and fulfillment of our journey in the universe and in time. The time has come to look again at the totality and to be what we were always meant to be: universal, total, spiritual beings. The hour for this vast synthesis, for a new encyclopedia of all our knowledge and the formulation of the agenda for our cosmic future has struck. Like the human eye which receives millions of bits of information at every glance, we must see the total picture and beauty of our planet, of the universe and of our lives.

Here again, science and rationalism have arrived at an impasse while religions have always seen the time dimension of our journey. What lessons religions can give geneticists, evolutionists and futurologists: the belief that our good deeds will be recorded and will contribute to a better humanity and a better future life (the genetic recording of the biologists); the belief that we are coming from somewhere and that we are going somewhere (evolutionists); the belief in a millennium, in a better, more peaceful world inspired and ruled by divine or cosmic laws, the belief that in us humans there are divine, cosmic elements which will flower to the point that we will become conscious of the total universe and that the universe will become conscious in ourselves (futurologists). As Catholics would say: the incarnated God, or Christ, is in all of us and for all of us to manifest.

What a formidable force it will be when all 4.5 billion humans on this planet have become spiritual beings in the eternal stream of time, conscious of the long-term consequences of their lives and actions and no longer prone to sacrifice these for petty, short-term interests and profit.

Here again an immense and beautiful responsibility behooves all Christian and religious teachers: it is no less than to prepare universal beings ready to flower and to fulfill their divine lives or cosmic destinies, as proclaimed by all great prophets for eons of time.

This brings me to the last but not the least segment of my world core curriculum.

IV. The Miracle of Individual Human Life

It is becoming increasingly clear in our debates on human rights that the individual is the alpha and omega of all our efforts. Individual human life is the highest form of universal or divine consciousness on our planet. Institutions, concepts, factories, systems, states, ideologies, theories have no consciousness. They are all servants, instruments, means for better lives and for the increase of individual human consciousness. We are faced today with the full-fledged centrality, divinity, dignity and miracle of individual human life as proclaimed relentlessly by Jesus, irrespective of race, sex, status, age, nation, physical or mental capacity: the divine nature of the human person.

Education of the newcomers is basically the teaching of the art of living and of human fulfillment within the immense knowledge of space and time acquired by humanity. It is to make each child feel like a king in the universe, an expanded being aggrandized by the vastness of our knowledge, which now reaches far into the infinitely large and the infinitely small, the distant past and the future. It is to make him feel proud to be a member of a transformed species whose eyesight, hearing, hands, legs, brain and heart have been multiplied a thousand times. Like the early Christians, the task is to help to maturity beings who exude a resplendent joy of living, who are witnesses to the beauty and majesty of creation. Knowledge, peace, happiness, goodness, love and meaningful lives—these must be the objectives of education.

And here I would complete my core curriculum for the individual with the four segments so dear to former Secretary-General U Thant:

— GOOD PHYSICAL LIVES:

   knowledge and care of the body
   teaching to see, to hear, to speak, to write, to observe, to create,
      to do, to use well all senses and physical capacities

— GOOD MENTAL LIVES:

   knowledge
   teaching to raise questions, to think, to analyze, to synthesize,
      to conclude, to communicate
   teaching to focus from the infinitely large to the infinitely small,
      from the distant past to the present and the future

— GOOD MORAL LIVES:

   teaching to love
   teaching truth, understanding, humility, liberty, reverence for
      life, compassion, altruism and service

— GOOD SPIRITUAL LIVES:

   spiritual exercises of interiority, meditation, prayer and commu-
      nion with God, the universe and eternity.

Here I have not much to say, for your knowledge and experience in these fields are far superior to mine. I tried in my book, *Most of All They Taught Me Happiness*, to summarize all I have learned on

the subject. Its starting point is this simple sentence by Norman
Cousins in the Preface, which I would like to see pondered by all
humans of this planet:

> The tragedy of life is not death, but what we let die inside us while
> we live.

Its epilogue is as follows:

> Decide to be happy
> render others happy
> proclaim your joy
> love passionately your miraculous life
> do not listen to promises
> do not wait for a better world
> be grateful for every moment of life
> switch on and keep on the positive buttons in yourself, those marked
>   optimism, serenity, confidence, positive thinking, love
> pray and thank God every day
> meditate—smile—laugh
> whistle—sing—dance
> look with fascination at everything
> fill you lungs and heart with liberty
> be yourself fully and immensely
> act like a king or queen unto Death
> feel God in your body, mind, heart, and soul
> and be convinced of eternal life and resurrection.

Conclusion

In all four segments of my proposed world curriculum, the spiritual visions of Christianity and other religions are truer, deeper and
more enriching than any purely rational, scientific, pragmatic, civilian education. Our lives and planet and human family advance in
time as a huge living ball of changes, interdependencies, dreams and
aspirations, the full significance and mystery of which will probably
forever escape us. But Christ gave us hope, faith and light. He gave
us his two great commandments: love the Father in heaven and love
each other with all your strength, all your mind, all your heart and
all your soul. His "holistic" and divinely simple teachings do in
many ways enrich the marvelous discoveries of science, reason, analysis and experimentation. But the latter are not all. There is more
in the heavens and on earth than in our discoveries. The unique

challenge to universal spiritual education is to integrate our vast scientific knowledge, our social knowledge, our knowledge of time and of the art of living into a shining, divine, blissful vision of our miraculous journey in the unfathomable universe.

Modern Christian and spiritual teachers could well say:

"Give me your children, and I will give them the heavens, happiness, the earth and immortality."

PART IV

My Personal Global Transcendence

PART IV

My Personal Global Experience

21

My Five Teilhardian Enlightenments

As far back as I can remember, the natural inclinations of my being have always been to love life, nature, people—especially old people, because they know so much—temples to God, sunshine, the stars, and the moon. My schoolmates used to laugh at me when I repeated my most basic conviction, namely, that life was *göttlich* or divine.

In my homeland of Alsace-Lorraine, then, I was taught that to be French or German was apparently more important than to be alive, for we were asked to give our lives for one or the other country. I learned that my grandfather had changed his nationality five times without leaving his village. I saw pictures of my father once in a German uniform, then in a French one. I was asked not to cross the Saar River, which I could see from my window. Then troops began to fill our region, fortifications were built, and twice our city was evacuated. The second time it meant war. Half of my family wore German uniforms, the other half French ones. I saw human horrors that were in utter contradiction to the beauty of nature, people, church, sunshine, the stars, the moon, and the cultures of Goethe and Racine.

After the war I decided to work for peace, and in 1948 I entered the United Nations. For the first years I worked there as an economist and I was privileged to be associated with some of the great ventures of the international community, such as the creation of the United Nations Development Program and the first world conferences. These pressed me constantly ahead toward a global view of our planet and its people.

In 1970, the year of the twenty-fifth anniversary of the UN, I was appointed director of the Secretary-General's Office. From then on I really had to have a total view and I often heard myself being described as a "Teilhardian." Father Emmanuel de Breuvery, a companion of Teilhard de Chardin, had already exposed me to the ideas and philosophy of Teilhard when I was working in the Natural Resources Division of the United Nations.[1] With Secretary-General U Thant, this exposure became ever more frequent, and now after a third of a century of service with the UN I can say unequivocally that much of what I have observed in the world bears out the all-encompassing, global, forward-looking philosophy of Teilhard de Chardin.

My own comprehension of the universal order of things took place progressively, at special moments of my life when I was challenged to explain what was going on in the world as seen from the UN. I like to call these moments my "Teilhardian enlightenments." They were all very pragmatic and arose from grass-roots observations of the world and of its people. As an economist, I had learned to observe, to analyze and to conclude. Nurtured by my love for life, for the world, the people, the moon, and the stars, a rather simple philosophy took form in me which has much in common with the vastly more prestigious cosmology of Teilhard de Chardin.

From the Infinitely Large to the Infinitely Small

The first enlightenment took place in 1973 when I was asked to speak to the American Association of Systems Analysts on the subject: "Can the United Nations become a functional system of world order?" It was on that occasion that I perceived and presented for the first time my Copernican view of world cooperation (see Part I, Chapter 3 above).

I was amazed by the simplicity of the pattern which was emerging from humanity's efforts as reflected in the United Nations. Everything was beginning to fall into place! A magnificent tapestry of our place in the universe was being woven by the world organization. A practical network of people and institutions all around the world was working on Pascal's genial view of the universe, from the infinitely large to the infinitely small. There remained a few gaps in the picture but soon they would be filled too.

[1] See *Most of All They Taught Me Happiness*, pp. 113–17.

This framework was typically Teilhardian. It was universal in scope and covered every aspect of our planetary home. Teilhard had viewed the UN as the nascent institutional embodiment of his vision. He did not live long enough to see today's formidable global enterprise of the United Nations, but the world organization reflects accurately the unified system of planetary concerns, aspirations, convergence and consciousness he had conceived.

A Biological View of Humanity

During the same year I was asked to speak at a meeting of the American Institute of Biological Sciences on "Biological Evolution and the United Nations." It was the time when the UN was embarking on the great conference on the seas and oceans. I remembered my discussions with Father de Breuvery on the astonishing, teeming biological resources of the seas and oceans. I decided therefore to speak on the UN's efforts, world conferences, and institutional arrangements in a number of major biological fields: the World Population Conference, the UN Conference on the Environment, the Law of the Sea Conference, the Habitat Conference, the Man and the Biosphere Program, etc., and I found myself suddenly exclaiming:

> "One could write a whole treatise about the birth of this collective brain and warning system of the human species. . . . All this forms part of a biological evolution. The human species continues to probe out, on an ever larger scale, the possibilities and limits of its terrestrial and perhaps tomorrow extraterrestrial habitat. This is one of the most thrilling and challenging periods of our planet's history. I am personally convinced that we will find the necessary adaptation of our brains, appetites, beliefs, feelings and behaviour to reach new equilibria and to select what is good for us instead of what is bad on our small spaceship Earth, circling in the universe, surrounded by its thin but so fantastically rich biosphere of only a few miles, containing all life of our solar system. . . ."[2]

After the speech, Professor Ernst Mayr, an anthropologist from Chicago University, commented that he had never heard the work of the UN presented in that way and that he felt he had witnessed a rare moment in evolution, namely, the birth of a new species, a metamorphosis similar to the transformation of the protozoa into

[2] Ibid., pp. 182–89.

metazoa. Perhaps indeed the human species was entering a new period of evolution, a period of planetary consciousness and global living, a fact that would be fully understood only by future generations.

If a Teilhardian had been in the audience, he would have stated most emphatically that my presentation was one long, practical illustration of Teilhard's philosophy of global evolution, of the noosphere, of metamorphosis, and of the birth of a collective brain to the human species! What was happening in the world and in the UN was just one vast confirmation of his vision. We did not have to wait for future generations to understand that we had entered the global age.

From the Infinite Past to the Infinite Future

For a couple of years I relied on these two "enlightenments" when presenting the work of the UN in my speeches and writings, and in taking further initiatives to fill the gaps in the two Copernican and biological schemes. It was not until 1975 that I made a new "find." I had been asked to speak at a joint conference of the Audubon Society and the Sierra Club on the subject "Interdependence: Societies' Interaction with Ecosystems."[3] I tried to do my best to show in a sweeping statement the main stages of our planet's evolution since its birth, our present position in time, and the recently emerging concerns about the future. Again, it was simply a schematic presentation of humanity's efforts and preoccupations as mirrored in the UN: the world agencies were increasingly called upon to deal with the past (preservation of the environment, of genetic resources, of the natural and cultural heritage), with the present (world conferences or international years on resources, water, desertification, science and technology, outer space, children, youth, women, the elderly, races, the handicapped, etc.) and with the future (development decades, climatic changes, Food 2000, Industry 2000, Education 2000, Health 2000, Environment 2000, etc.).

The world had never seen anything like it! But what was happening was in reality very simple: the human species, as a result of its

[3] The speech was published in "Earthcare, Global Protection of Natural Areas," edited by Edmond Schoffield, Westview Press, Boulder, Colorado, 1980 (pp. 583–98).

expanding knowledge, intelligence and discoveries, was suddenly forced to visualize the entire time span of our planet, reaching from our most distant astrophysical and paleontological past to the remaining six to eight billion years of our future. As a matter of fact, each layer of our Copernican reality has a time dimension, from our planet's total duration to the length of a human life, down to the infinitely brief span of an atomic particle. Moreover, everything we are doing today has a potentially lasting effect on the future.

Our planet was a teeming ball of incredible interdependencies, complexities, intensities, relationships, exchanges, streams, flows and long-term changes, floating and evolving in the universe, carrying on its crust a species which had suddenly been able to dissect, unlock, and analyze most of that fantastic reality, and which was beginning to change it in the most far-reaching fashion. What was needed was no less than a total earth science in space and in time, a science of all interdependencies, a view of the earth and of humans as one evolving entity, and a new art of planetary management and caretaking of which the first rudiments were being born right under our eyes in the world organizations.

That speech brought me one step closer to Teilhard's theory of evolution, to his view of the earth as a "living cell" as well as his outcry for responsible earth management. Teilhard had drawn his vision from his work as an archaeologist, paleontologist and evolutionary scientist. I had drawn mine from my practical observations in humanity's first planetary institutions.

A Spiritual Dimension

Two years later, in 1977, a new broadening of my views took place. The religion taught me during my youth had largely given way to the rationalism, scientism and intellectualism so prevalent in our time. I was not at all concerned with spirituality and religion in the United Nations. But as a close collaborator of U Thant, I could not fail to be deeply impressed by his view that, of all human values, the spiritual ones were the highest. I became accustomed to his familiar fourfold presentation of all human values and concerns. I also discovered that Dag Hammarskjöld, the rational Nordic economist, had ended up as a mystic. He too held at the end of his life that spirituality was the ultimate key to our earthly fate.

About that time the UN Meditation Group and the various

religions accredited to the UN asked me to speak about the spirituality of our Secretaries-General and of the UN. I noted that during most of its existence the UN had dealt primarily with the immediate, physical, material and mental needs of humanity (avoidance of war, hunger, health, education, etc.). But I had already seen the UN's scope vastly expand into space and into time. Was the UN taking moreover the path of all religions which dealt with the total human person in the total universe and total time? Was it not inevitable that the UN would sooner or later also acquire a spiritual dimension, once the other priorities of life (physical, mental and moral) had been met (*primum vivere, deinde philosophari*)?

I suddenly understood U Thant's belief that the world would be a good place to live in only when its billions of people understood that they were part of total creation; that the goodness of humanity depended on their individual goodness and internal purity; that our lives were not closed at the beginning and the end but were part of an endless stream. Then I understood Hammarskjöld, who ultimately referred for enlightenment all human problems to a greater, outside judge—to God. Then I understood better the visits of Pope Paul VI and John Paul II to the United Nations and their plea to nations to repeat their tremendous scientific and material achievements in the fields of the heart and the soul. The lawyer-economist I had been for so many years joined their ranks, for I had not received from law and economics the proper answers to the problems of life and death and of our meaning in the universe.

I have come to believe firmly today that our future peace, justice, fulfillment, happiness and harmony on this planet will not depend on world government but on divine or cosmic government, meaning that we must seek and apply the "natural," "evolutionary," "divine," "universal" or "cosmic" laws which must rule our journey in the cosmos. Most of these laws can be found in the great religions and prophecies, and they are being rediscovered slowly but surely in the world organizations.

Any Teilhardian will recognize in this the spiritual transcendence which he announced so emphatically as the next step in our evolution. He had arrived at this conclusion from both his archaeological and his theological studies. I had arrived at mine through three decades of observation and endeavors in our planet's first universal organization.

The Human Cosmos and Happiness

Accustomed now to deal with broad global problems in time and in space, and increasingly drawn by my work to universal and philosophical concepts, I needed to retain a firmer root on earth, a more immediate, concrete, tangible challenge. I found it in a question which increasingly returned to my mind. "What is in it for me? What does this all mean for the individual human person?" Creation, the universe, remote stars, the earth, spirituality and eternity are terribly big words compared with my tiny self. As an antidote to cosmic dimensions and vagueness, I began to concentrate on my own personal life, dreams, experiences, past, family, as well as on circumstances and persons who had played an important role or left a lasting impression on me. I asked myself the question: "Suppose I die tomorrow? What are the lessons I would like to leave behind, especially for my children and grandchildren?"

The answer was clear: I had to find out by recording the most sensitive highlights of my life, be it persons, events, personal conclusions or important turning points. Since my heavy duties at the UN prevented me from writing a comprehensive, well-structured work with a beginning and an end, I decided to write down my lessons from life in the form of anecdotes and stories. There were about fifty of them. When they were finished, I discovered that there was one constant thread, theme or search running through all of them: the quest for happiness.

I had always sought the maximum fulfillment of my "divine" life! I had been on the constant lookout for circumstances, examples and people who would help me perfect the art of living. I discovered that for me life had always been the highest value, a sacred gift. I had been given the incredible privilege of opening for a few years my eyes, ears, mind, heart and soul to the stupendous creation and the world around me. I had walked through the festival of life with the wondrous eyes of a child. I had lived and loved my life with every fiber of my heart, with true enthusiasm (by God possessed). And that realization gave me the clue to my place in the total scheme: the universe is made up of endless cosmoses, from the infinitely large to the infinitely small: I am one of these cosmoses, linked with everything in the heavens and on earth, endowed with a unique and unrepeatable life in all eternity, were it only because the external circumstances and companions would never be the same. How did the world at the precise moment of time when my human cosmos was inserted in it look? How did I relate to it? How did I find fulfillment in it?

Obviously it was a highly imperfect world, in which two thirds of humanity still lived in utter poverty while hundreds of billions of dollars were being squandered each year on frightful armaments. It was a highly immoral world, a largely non-spiritual world, seemingly abandoned by God to an unknown fate in the universe. I had seen all its evils, injustices, contradictions, and follies during a World War and during my thirty-three years of world service. Could I despair? Should I give up? Was the universe an immense nonsense?

No, because I was human, that is, endowed with the highest privileges and perceptions of any living species on this planet; it was up to me to sharpen these admirable instruments called doing, seeing, hearing, thinking, feeling, dreaming, hoping and loving; I could focus my attention and love from a flower or a person to the universe and God, from the infinite past to the infinite future; I could profit from the incredible expansion of my hands, arms, legs, eyes, ears and brain through science and technology; I could seek, know and feel in myself the entire universe and Godhead, for I was part of them and they were part of me; it could not be otherwise; and last but not least I was the master of my cosmos, it was up to me to guide it, to uplift it, to give it confidence and joy, to keep it in an endless, wondrous, inquisitive, searching, loving and hopeful mood. If I visualize myself as a little erect being on the surface of our whirling planet Earth among billions of other humans, I am not more than a tiny speck. And yet that speck can embrace the heavens, the earth, humanity, the past, present and future! It can be and it is an active actor and receptor of the entire universe. To be this "fullest being" is our cosmic task on earth, our sacred, spiritual duty. And to do that I don't have to wait until the whole world is perfect. Indeed, I can contribute right away my peace, goodness and happiness to the human family.

And when I die, it will by no means be the end: my matter and life will become other matter and life; my thoughts, actions and feelings will remain part of the total stock of thoughts, actions and feelings of humanity; there will have been only a change of worlds. Even after the explosion of our solar system into fathomless space, every atom of this planet will again become an atom or another star, as it has been and will be for all eternity. No, I would never understand it all, I would not even understand a small part of it, and yet to be alive, to feel it, to know what I know, to be admitted to the banquet of life on our miraculous planet was indeed a fantastic privilege, a mysterious, stupendous phenomenon or gift of God in the vast unfathomable universe.

And I wondered why all my human relatives in the affluent world did not have the same elation about life, why they did not share my enthusiasm and gratitude, why they did not consider life as great, sacred, untouchable and divine; why there was war, killing, hurting and constant debasing of life; why there was so much injustice, pessimism and lamenting; why they did not help their poor fellow humans in the Third World; why we did not all love up to the brim our beautiful planet, our skies, our waters, our mountains, our seas, our brethren the animals, our sisters the flowers, our vast human family with its teeming diversity and dreams, down to each individual miraculous, unique human being; why we did not like, observe, penetrate our self, shudder at its divine, mysterious greatness; feel God and the universe in ourselves and make shine to maximum intensity the star which each of us is in creation.

Well, even if humanity did not have its values straight and believed that wealth, power, arms, glory, a nation, a race, a religion, a business or an ideology were superior to life, I would carry the jewel of my own life preciously and unscathed through the noisy market place. Even if I was alone of the four and a half billion people of this planet who believed in the superiority, sanctity and divinity of life (and I am not alone), I would proclaim and practice this truth fearlessly, joyously and proudly to the very end, be it in prison or at the top of the United Nations.

And once more, as I arrived at these conclusions, the image of Teilhard de Chardin came back to me. This time it was not as a philosophical concept or vision, but the image of his person as described in a wonderful story by Jean Houston. As a young girl, Jean used to cross Central Park in New York on the way to school. She often met in the park an elderly gentleman, who was either sitting on a bench or walking around. She talked to him and they became friends. The gray-haired gentleman seemed constantly afloat in a strange, endless, joyous astonishment at life. He would hold a flower or an insect in his hand and infer from it the whole universe and story of creation and evolution. As William Blake said:

> *To see the world in a grain of sand,*
> *And a heaven in a wild flower;*
> *Hold infinity in the palm of your hand,*
> *And eternity in an hour.*

The old gentleman had introduced himself and was known to Jean Houston as Mr. Teller, but years later, when she studied philosophy and saw a picture of Teilhard de Chardin, she exclaimed: "But this is Mr. Teller, my friend, the old gentleman in the park!"

And Fate wanted it to be that she arranged the publication of my little life stories and essays on human happiness!

At this juncture of my life, after a long, meandering search for truth, the picture I have obtained from the United Nations' global observation tower is now pretty clear. The table of contents of a new world encyclopedia is ready. The agenda for the next chapter of humanity is in sight. But this is when the real Teilhardian period begins: with this vast fundamental, well-ordered knowledge on hand we must now administer our planet well, learn the art of peaceful, personal and social living, practice justice, love and tolerance, and celebrate the miracle of life through individual peace, happiness, joy, altruism and harmony in the endless stream of changing worlds. Our new global living is so sudden, so complex, so manifold and mind-boggling, it is such a mixture of small and big, global and local, past and future, young and old, that our bewilderment and anxiety are not surprising, but rather normal. To humanity I would simply say: do not despair, but learn.

We must now prepare for a Bimillennium Celebration of Life, free of war, violence, hunger and despair; a world in which every child can keep and nourish his inborn love for life, nature, people, God, sunshine, the stars, the moon and so many other wonderful things.

22

How I Became a Spiritual Being[1]

In [your book] Most of All They Taught Me Happiness, *you wrote four chapters on U Thant, telling how he influenced your spiritual life. It is surprising how a man of a Buddhist tradition had more effect on your spirituality than someone like Thomas Merton. How do you explain this?*

I can explain this, and I feel my experience can be of value to others because it is not an infrequent one. I have never been a deeply religious person. I was raised in a good Catholic family, but for long in my life, I had never met anyone who inspired me to become a really spiritual person. Our schools in France have practically eradicated religion. Intelligence and performance are the highest virtues. As a young person, I obviously followed the prevailing ideas and values of my time and tried to do my best within their realm. At the university it was the same story. I then came to work for the United Nations where the highest virtue is not spirituality but again high intelligence and performance. Our whole world seems to be like that. One's life is unavoidably dominated by the values of the time. Of course, one prays, one goes to church and one raises the children in one's faith, but for me there has never been anything deeper than that. My readings were always in economics, politics and law. I had never found Thomas Merton included in the requirements of my reading lists.

At the age of forty-six I became director of Secretary-General U Thant's office. Here, for the first time in my life, I met a person who

[1] A Message of Hope from an Optimist at the United Nations, interview with Sister Mary Madden, C.S.J. published in the magazine *Sisters Today*, October 1979.

inspired me, a man who was deeply religious, who had a profound spirituality and code of human ethics which he applied to every moment and situation of his day. This I had never experienced. I had met people with very beautiful ideas about spirituality who did not practice what they preached. Here was a man who never spoke badly about anyone else—and God knows how many occasions he had for it!—who was always patient, widely open to others, never vainglorious, proud or demanding. To the humblest being he was most respectful and a friend. The UN guards remember him well for his immense human kindness. As one of them put it: "He could have the President of the United States waiting for him, but the first thing he would do would be to greet the guard who opened the door. Then, he would ask how you were, no matter who was there. He was one of the most marvelous human beings I ever met in my life."[2]

As I became more and more amazed at the authenticity of this man and of his actions in everyday life, I began to discuss religion with him. I tried to understand him better and found that he was simply, honestly and painstakingly applying his Buddhist faith to daily life. He was far from being a mystic like Hammarskjöld, who was in constant negotiation with God. I discovered that for U Thant there was no difference between spirituality, religion and life. Life was for him a constant spirituality. I studied Buddhism to understand him better. We became great friends. He was able to teach me what my Catholic priests had always told me, but at that time I hadn't listened. Here, in the middle of my life, was the master, the one who inspired me, someone I could imitate like a father. This has changed my life. Perhaps what we need most at this time are masters who give us the good example. And, like U Thant, they ought to include people in highest office and with wide responsibilities. All statesmen should be models and masters for their people, human beings with a deep philosophy, ethics and spirituality, as were Dag Hammarskjöld and U Thant at the UN.

From the moment I became interested in the spiritual dimension of life, everything started to change. I began to read Hammarskjöld's *Markings*. I discovered that he had found God as the Master and that he had to interpret His will as the Secretary-General of the United Nations. His preferred authors were Thomas à Kempis and

2 UN Meditation Group, *A Salute to the UN Security and Safety Service* (Garden City, N.Y.: Agni Press, 1977), pp. 90–91.

St. John of the Cross, whom I had never read in my life. I began to read the mystics and understood much more about this new dimension of life consciousness. Some religious people began to be interested in my ideas. I was invited to participate in an East-West monastic encounter. There I discovered Merton and began to read his works. Before that I had never heard of him.

Later on I was made a member of the East-West Monastic Board because its members wanted to know what was going on in the world organization. I am learning a great deal from them and they are also learning from me. I found that most monastic orders are organized on the basis of U Thant's cherished four categories of human needs and qualities: physical, mental, moral and spiritual. I learned that he was a monk himself. Buddhists are required to go to a monastery for one month each year. Since he could not go back to a Burmese monastery, he acted as a kind of monk in the United Nations, the same way as Hammarskjöld acted as a solitary mystic in it. This has been a tremendous experience for me, and as a result I have been writing more and more about the need for spirituality as an answer to our personal as well as world problems. I would like the whole world to benefit from my experience and to derive the same enlightenment, happiness, serenity and hope in the future as I derived from my contact with U Thant. I would never have thought that I would discover spirituality in the United Nations! The same happened to the Western, rational, hyperintellectual Dag Hammarskjöld. It is a subject which therefore merits close attention. Perhaps spirituality is such a fundamental human need that it always reappears in one form or another in life and throughout history and that we are about to witness now its renaissance in a global, planetary context.[3]

[3] I am glad that Professor Ewert Cousins, head of the Fordham University Spirituality Program, has entrusted one of his students with the preparation of a thesis on the spirituality of Dag Hammarskjöld and U Thant.

23

A Proclamation of Faith

I am often asked why the United Nations occupies such an important part in my writings. There are two reasons for it: first, the United Nations has helped me to extend tremendously my consciousness of the world and of humanity. It has played for my comprehension of planet Earth and of its people the same role that thought, prayer and meditation later played for the understanding of my inner world. Secondly, there can be no doubt that the main condition for world happiness and spirituality is peace, for it is in peace only that we will be able to enjoy happiness, fully flower as human beings, and fulfill our cosmic destiny. A strengthened and actively supported United Nations can help enormously in attaining peace, human fulfillment and a better understanding of our fate. The horrid sufferings and destruction I saw as a young man during World War II could have been avoided if the people had worked harder for a strong and universal League of Nations. Adventures like those of Hitler and Mussolini might have been impossible.

I have seen the United Nations grow and greatly change since I joined it a third of a century ago. It has taught me more than any school or university on earth. It has taught me in particular to be confident in humankind's capacity to organize itself in peace, justice and happiness on our little planet. We are scarcely emerging from the political cave age. We are only in the kindergarten of the global school. Therefore, despite the frustrations and pitfalls I have known, after so many years of world service, I am today more enthusiastic than ever about the United Nations. I want to communicate this enthusiasm to the people, for nothing is more important for our future than public understanding and support for the world's first universal organization.

When I remember the sufferings and waste I saw in Europe during my youth, I cannot help feeling that humanity has covered an immense distance, that we are finally on the right road and that we will never again see a world war on this planet. For a third of a century now, all children in Europe could go to sleep every night without having to fear a war the next morning. The political wisdom achieved in Europe will now extend also to the rest of the world. We will see dialogue and cooperation progressively replace everywhere conflicts and confrontations. Someday the last decades of the twentieth century will be remembered as one of the greatest turning points in human history.

True enough, there remain immense problems, there could be less horrid nonsense, more peace and a better organization than the UN, but we have passed successfully through one of the most colossal and complex periods of change in all human evolution without slaughtering each other on a mass scale. This augurs well for the future and, since I have been privileged to work for one of the most exciting and most misunderstood organizations on earth, I wish to declare unambiguously my profound faith in the United Nations and bear witness to the human progress it represents, despite all its shortcomings, failures and errors. If someone had told me thirty years ago that I would see the degree of international cooperation and world convergence I see today, I would not have believed it. It is therefore only fitting that I proclaim my faith in an organization which will be considered someday as the paradigm of the new millennium.

Briefly, here are my articles of faith in the UN:

The UN has
- helped one billion people gain independence with a minimum of bloodshed, thus completing the historical movement started two hundred years ago by the Declaration of Independence;
- helped the emergence of the poorer countries into the modern age, providing a safety lid for the explosive feelings of our less fortunate brethren at the injustices which prevail in the world;
- provided a talking place and a meeting ground during the worst periods of the cold war;
- provided for the first time in history a code of ethics for rela-

tions between the most powerful entities on earth: armed nations;

— prevented, by its mere existence, even more national political and military adventures;

— provided a covering lid for hot conflicts, a standstill for fighting, a separation of belligerents and a talking ground between them;

— fared better with any conflict brought before it than unilateral, forceful attempts at settlement;

— been a moral force for progress toward political maturity, defusion of tensions, better understanding and reason around the world, proving that talking and listening are the beginning of wisdom and peace in human relations;

— been a platform for the expression and defense of all basic human aspirations, including those of liberty, equality and fraternity proclaimed by the American and French Revolutions on the eve of the modern age;

— enhanced immensely a planetary acceptance of the racial equality of all human beings;

— warned humanity of the immorality, inhumanity, dangers and inacceptability of armaments;

— warned humankind of its global limits and environmental constraints;

— progressively developed a functional system of world order, covering with its large number of specialized agencies and programs practically every field of human concern.

The UN is

— the first universal, global instrument humanity has ever had;

— the best chance of governments and nations to remain the permanent political and administrative units of planet Earth, provided they use and make the UN work to the satisfaction of the people;

— the place where new ethical values for nations and humanity are being formulated;

— the greatest universal collective effort ever attempted to reduce and eradicate all forms of violence from this planet;

— the best chance to keep within bounds new forms of excessive power and to develop codes of conduct for them;

— the central, permanent meeting ground of all human aspira-

tions in which will be molded a peaceful, just, safe and happy future for the human race;
— a treasure chest of world information;
— an incipient brain of the human species, registering global dangers and tendencies, keeping world conditions and phenomena under constant review, and fostering a better knowledge of our planet's resources and contraints;
— an incipient world nervous system which relays global findings and warnings to governments, local collectivities and the peoples;
— an incipient conscience and heart of humanity, which speaks for what is good and against what is bad for humans; which advocates and fosters understanding, cooperation and altruism instead of division, struggle and indifference among nations;
— an observatory into the future, since most problems facing humankind will derive from the expansion of the human race and its massive transformation of the physical and living conditions of our planet;
— an international mechanism born at the precise moment when humanity is becoming one global, complex, interdependent entity in so many respects; this will be its greatest historical chance of success and usefulness to the human race;
— the beginning of an important new story in evolution: the story of humanity as one family or one society living in one common home.

The UN should
— never be by-passed by any nation or group of nations as humanity's peacekeeping force;
— be used faithfully, in accordance with the Charter and the pledge of compliance by each member government, for the settlement of conflicts and the maintenance and strengthening of world peace;
— be further strengthened and perfected as a warning tower for global trends and menaces;
— be further developed as the planet's central data bank;
— be strengthened regionally, bringing each continent to bear its full contribution and role in the total world order;
— never be by-passed as the forum for the consideration of any problems which are of a world-wide nature and of concern to all humans;

— strengthen its links with the world scientific and academic community. The United Nations University and the University of Peace constitute, in this respect, major historical steps forward in world cooperation and human evolution;

— strengthen its links with the world's religions, since humanity will now enter its moral and spiritual age;

— further elaborate its cosmic vision by adding to its present physical, mental and moral comprehension a spiritual, mystical dimension of our mysterious journey in the universe.

Governments should

— respect, support, strengthen and constantly improve their first planetary instrument for world peace, justice, progress, diagnosis, cooperation, forecasting and management; fulfill faithfully their obligations toward the Charter, a fact which alone would bring about peace, order and understanding in the world;

— implement the recommendations of the UN, above all by putting an end to the obsolete, insane and wasteful armaments race;

— teach our children and youth about the global age, global living and the global intergovernmental instruments which have been created to help cope with global problems;

— enlist the impatience, idealism and energy of youth in building a better world, free of war, want, hatred and injustice;

— join their efforts in unprecedented ways to better explore, utilize and conserve the resources of our planet;

— promote a real revolution in world cooperation for the common benefit of the whole human race;

— better inform and educate the people about the work and efforts of the UN and its specialized agencies, thereby giving them confidence that something is being done about the problems which confront humankind on a global scale;

— enlist the support and better understanding of parliamentarians for a world cooperation which is of direct interest and consequence to their electorates;

— turn their eyes away from the past and direct them to the future;

— plan for the arrival of a few billion more people on this planet;

— extend their vision and concern to the whole planet, to all peoples and to all future generations instead of seeing, defending and promoting only narrow, immediate and transient national interests.

The people should
— have faith in the future and give a chance to the most noble attempt at world peace and cooperation ever undertaken on this planet;
— take an interest in the UN, its peacekeeping and peacemaking activities, its specialized agencies, its organs, its information, its studies, its meetings, its recommendations, its publications, its programs, its world conferences, its international years and its emerging global vision;
— support, join or create volunteer groups or associations for the UN in order to be better informed about the efforts of *their* UN, and discuss the issues before it;
— celebrate United Nations Day on October 24;
— display the UN flag;
— pray for the UN;
— request that children be educated about the UN and the world's global problems, which affect every citizen;
— demand from the news media more information about the UN, its specialized agencies, global problems and efforts for peace, justice and a better world;
— request their political representatives to take a greater interest in world cooperation and development, which have become affairs of concern to all peoples;
— inform themselves of the efforts of the more than ten thousand international non-governmental organizations which in a vast number of professional, humanitarian and scientific fields foster international cooperation, friendship and common concerns;[1]
— act and behave in greater cognizance of the fact that, in a world of several billion people, peace, progress, justice, understanding and spirituality are essentially the sum total of the peace, progress, justice, understanding and spirituality of all individuals.

Religions should
— take an active interest in the work and efforts of the UN and inform their members properly about them;

[1] The UN has entrusted to the Union of International Associations the publication of a Yearbook of International Organizations. See "Networking," by Jessica Lynack and Jeffrey Stamps, (Doubleday, 1982), Chapter 9, pp. 189–205.

— accelerate their ecumenism and create common world religious institutions which would bring the resources and inspirations of the religions to bear upon the solution of world problems;

— display the UN flag in all their houses of worship;

— pray and organize world prayers for the UN and for all peacemakers;

— pray God for our successful passage into the global age without a war or a nuclear holocaust.

24

My Creed in Human Happiness

As I near the end of my journey on planet Earth, may I dare to offer a few personal conclusions regarding the quest for human happiness:

I believe that happiness is

> *love for the heavens*
> *love for our beautiful planet*
> *love for all humankind*
> *love for my family*
> *love for my work*
> *love for my miraculous life*

I believe that happiness is

> *a personal decision*
> *an internal readiness*
> *the supreme harmony between senses, mind,*
>   *heart and soul*

I believe that happiness is

> *the greatest form of freedom*
> *the ultimate fulfillment of life*
> *the highest transcendence of life*
> *a powerful self-assertion*

I believe that happiness

> *is reached through physical, mental, moral and*
>   *spiritual care and exercises*

I believe that happiness can be achieved

> *through concentration upon oneself*
> *opening oneself to others*
> *elevating oneself to God*

I believe that happiness is

> *to look always at the good side of life*
> *to be in constant amazement and reverence for life*
> *to be passionate about life*
> *to be enthusiastic about life*

I believe that happiness is better than gloom

> *optimism better than pessimism*
> *hope better than despair*
> *confidence better than diffidence*
> *positive thinking better than negative thinking*
> *a smile better than a frown*
> *cleanliness better than impurity*
> *cooperation better than obstruction*
> *friendship better than hostility*
> *truth better than falsehood*
> *love better than hatred*
> *altruism better than egotism*
> *peace better than conflict*
> *serenity better than anxiety*

I believe that happiness is

> *the ultimate objective of life*
> *a sacred duty of the living*
> *an act of grace for the miraculous gift of life*

I believe that happiness is

> *to lead good physical lives*
> *to constantly broaden one's knowledge*
> *to live in peace and friendship with all our human*
>   *brethren and sisters*
> *to lead a pure inner life in harmony with*
>   *God, humanity, our planet, the universe and eternity*

I believe that happiness

> *brings health and serenity*
> *unlocks the mind*
> *broadens the heart*
> *brings us near to God and to cosmic understanding*

I believe that happiness

> *is the secret of life and youth*
> *the human answer to many insoluble questions*
> *the lamp that illuminates our amazing journey in*
> *   the vast, incomprehensible universe.*

25

Conclusion

O God, forgive me all this multitude of words which are so feeble to express my love for the greatness of Your creation. As if they were not enough—and they will never be enough—I wish to let upwell a few final waves of ecstasy.

Dear God,

Humanity has achieved marvelous successes since the advent of its scientific and industrial age. It has unlocked many secrets and mysteries of nature and of the universe. It has penetrated into every possible aspect of the infinite manifestations of Your creation. It has transcended its physical and sensory capacities to the point of becoming a different species. It has been able to accommodate thousands of millions more people in the flow of human life on this planet. It has provided for longer lives, better lives and vastly improved knowledge for large numbers of people. It has eradicated most epidemics and diseases afflicting human life. It has conquered many social inequalities and evils in human relations. It has elevated itself from a passive species dominated by nature and its environment to an active living entity able to transform, mold, manage and improve planet Earth for its flowering.

Despite all the wars, mistakes, injustices and follies of power and armaments, this has been a prodigious period of human ascent which will stand out as one of the greatest advances in our evolution. We must be thankful to You, O God, for having allowed us to transcend our physical and mental nature into such knowledge and mastery. Men and women of science who have pierced the surrounding reality and provided the basis for our conquests deserve our deepest gratitude.

But we are now entering a new age, the understanding and image of which still remain to be charted. After more than thirty years of observation and thinking from the balcony of world history at the United Nations, may I offer these suggestions and hopes for our passage into the first planetary civilization:

— It is high time for humanity to accept and to work out the full consequences of the total global and interdependent nature of our planetary home and of our species. Our survival and further progress will depend largely on the advent of global visions and of proper global education in all countries of the world.

— We must effectuate a giant leap forward into the future and henceforth see ourselves and our actions in the endless stream of time.

— There is a pressing need for a science and art of planetary management and therapy which will recognize the potentialities as well as the limits of our planet for the improvement of human life; higher global education must provide well-prepared, responsible world managers, caretakers and leaders for government, religions, firms, international organizations and transnational entities.

— While continuing to learn more about our planet and its proper management, we must now pass from the national to the planetary age and from the rational to the moral and spiritual age. We must reinsert ourselves into the total visions of the great religions and prophets. Science must take its appropriate place in these greater visions which alone can provide satisfactory answers to the mysteries of life, of the universe and of right human relations.

— The world's major religions must speed up dramatically their ecumenical movement and recognize the unity of their objectives in the diversity of their cults. Religions must actively cooperate to bring to unprecedented heights a better understanding of the mysteries of life and of our place in the universe. "My religion, right or wrong," and "My nation, right or wrong" must be abandoned forever in the planetary age.

— Since the world's religions, governments, enterprises and international organizations all work to achieve the greatest possible happiness of people, they must join their forces and cooperate actively in order to bring about a happy, just, peaceful, prosperous and godly society on earth.

— Individual as well as collective life must be elevated from the purely material and intellectual planes to the higher summits of morality (right human relations) and spirituality (right relations with God, creation, infinity and eternity). Humans in all walks of life must contribute maximum physical, mental, moral and spiritual lives to humanity's total life. Scientists and intellectuals must strive for moral and spiritual excellence. Religious and spiritual people must appreciate and be cognizant of scientific achievements.

— Humanity must bring into full play the forces of the "mystery of faith," of hope, of belief in human life, in the progress of humanity, in greater civilization, in further evolution, in the accomplishment of a divine design. Religious and spiritual people must teach the world actively about the mystery of faith, of interiority, of mysticism, of prayer and meditation and of the happiness derived from spiritual beliefs and exercises.

— Infinitely more attention must be accorded to the great, simple and so effective concepts of love, peace, compassion, truth, purity, goodness, humility, faith, divinity, the heart, the soul, resurrection, infinity and eternity. They must become the luminous pillars of human civilization in a global, universal context.

— Now must dawn a world-wide era of supreme reverence for life, embodied in a universal, peaceful, non-violent, disarmed, just society as heralded by all great religious leaders. We must work out the rules of world harmony between all peoples, between humanity and the earth, and between humanity and the divine.

— The supreme unity of the human family, universal and interdependent, as seen by all great religions must now become a political reality; the hour has struck for the implementation of a spiritual vision of world affairs; the next great task of humanity will be to determine the divine or cosmic laws which must rule our behavior on this planet.

— We must establish a vast inventory of all our knowledge and rank everything at its right place in the universal scheme that has been revealed to us; we must rejoice at our progress and achievements and raise our sights to further objectives and summits to be attained.

— We must learn to work in common and to unite our wills,

dreams, intelligence and resources towards the fashioning of a world permitting the fullest flowering of human life everywhere.

— We must learn to adjust our individual and group interests to the supreme interests, survival and apotheosis of the human race.

— We must strive to become a majority, nay, a unanimity, of positive, hopeful, enthusiastic, life-impassioned, universe- and divinity-enamored beings.

— We must learn to refrain from exploiting and developing the negative sides of our discoveries.

— We must learn to foresee intelligently the world-wide and long-term consequences of our policies and actions, and outgrow the present primitive age of learning by accident and burning our fingers like ignorant little children.

— We must define a new world ethics.

— We must respect and love each other as unique, unrepeatable, sacrosanct miracles in the universe and in eternity.

— From the evolutionary stage of perfectly coordinated, well-adapted individual beings, we must now pass to the next stage of a perfectly coordinated, well-adapted, harmonious human society.

— We must learn to become responsible members of a newly born global family endowed with common institutions, a common brain, heart, nervous system and soul geared to our common survival and flowering on planet Earth; we must help this latest-formed and greatest entity achieve its maximum harmonious functioning and perfection within our planet's given endowment.

— We must learn to focus easily and lovingly our minds, hearts, senses and souls over the entire gamut of creation, from the infinitely large to the infinitely small, from the stars to the flowers of the earth, from the entire human family to the last of our sisters and brethren, embracing at any moment the plenitude of the miracle of creation and of being.

— We must help enhance the biological and divine law of unity in diversity in all realms of creation, from science to culture, from the human family to the individual, from God-the-unique to God-the-infinitely-diverse in the endless manifestations of matter and life.

— As the religions have done for thousands of years, we must teach humans to see at all times their right place in the universe, in the eternal flow of time, on our planet and in our human family. Ours will stand out as the epoch of most gigantic comprehension, synthesis, elevation and pacification there ever was.

— We must plan now for the year 2000 a Bimillennium Celebration of Life, the advent of an Era of Peace, of a Golden Age, of the First Millennium of World Harmony and Human Happiness in which our globe will become a showcase in the universe, a true miracle of divine fulfillment, a model of peace, justice, humaneness, love, kindness and joy in the fathomless expanses of creation.

26

Meditation

Whenever I am sad or in despair or in rebellion against the state of human affairs, all I need to do is to think of You, O God, the Father, the Creator, and all becomes bright again. "He who follows Me," said the Christ, "walks not in darkness, for he will have the light of life." From the summit of the divine, all falls into place. My unhappiness, despair or complaints become so tiny and irrelevant in the total order of things. I need You, O God and Your endless, manifold incarnations in the beauty of creation. I need You to elevate me above my miserable, ephemeral condition and concerns. I need You to give me light, faith and hope. I need You to show me the reason and beauty of the universe. I need You to give sense and purpose to my life which so often appears to me meaningless.

We humans are a great species, undoubtedly endowed with a divine nature or spark, but we shall never be able to pierce the ultimate mysteries of the universe and of life. The totality of creation and of time, the infinitely large and the infinitely small, the beginningless beginning and the endless end will forever escape us. The more we know, the less we understand the totality. Scientists can see no end to time and space. Perhaps it is all very simple, infinitely more simple than we all think, but we are not made to understand it. Hence the need to believe in You as a great, simple, limitless power, an all-encompassing mind, an all-embracing heart, an all-pervading soul endowed with all the perfections we seek on earth. Even if You didn't exist, we would have to invent You as did so many cultures and civilizations over the millennia. There must be a profound reason for You. You are as alive and indispensable today as at any other period of our journey. Once again You are the light in the darkness, the answer to our anxiety, the image of our future. Strangely and significantly enough, we have endowed You with the ultimate perfection of our senses, incapable as we are to perceive You otherwise than as we see ourselves ideally in the universe. Yes, be it You as one God or as a God in the multiple manifestations of creation, You are the ultimate, simple, glorious, reassuring, all-satisfying answer to our unpierceable mysteries. I cannot prove it? Well, when I am sad or in despair or in rebellion, I think of You and all becomes bright again: a smile appears on my face, a light shines in my eyes, a warm flood of happiness inundates my heart, a wonderful leaven elevates my entire being. I am happy, consoled, hopeful again, more joyful to be alive: the miracle of faith has operated once more. You have touched me with Your invisible, unprovable hand. This is good enough proof for me as well as for hundreds of millions of brothers and sisters on this planet. The miracle of faith is so effective, so powerful, so extraordinary, even and especially in the face of adversity, sickness and death, that humans who do not use it are simply to be pitied. It is difficult to understand that so many people can live with their eyes glued to the material and mental only, disregarding the immensity and beauty of the spiritual. And what is true of the individual is also true of a society and of the entire human family: we must re-establish You at the center of our lives and of all our efforts, we must try to better understand Your great scheme and design. We must turn to You to see right, to feel right, to think right and to manage rightly our planet and our future destiny.

Yes, we must join our Hindu brethren and call henceforth our planet "Brahma" or the Planet of God.

27

Final Prayer and New Genesis

O God, I do not know who You are, but I am in exultant joy before the magnificence of Your creation.

O God, I do not know why You gave me life, but I thank You with every fiber of my heart for having lit up in me the divine spark of light in the vast, incomprehensible universe.

O God, I know that I come from You, that I am part of You, that I will return to You, and that there will be no end to my rebirth in the eternal stream of Your splendid creation.

O God, I do not know why You created light and darkness, happiness and despair, good and evil, love and hatred, creation and destruction, matter and void, and allowed us to choose constantly between the two, but I know that it is my duty and joy to throw down my gauntlet for light, brightness, compassion, goodness, happiness, truthfulness, life, beauty and love.

O God, only You know the meaning of all there is in the heavens and on earth. Why don't You return again to tell us once more what our lives and destiny should truly be?

O God, I cannot define You, I cannot see You, I cannot perceive You, I cannot understand You, I cannot embrace You, but I can most definitely feel You, love You and know that You are.

Please, O God, have pity on us and allow us to become at long last a warless, weaponless, hungerless, horrorless, just, kind, truthful, thankful, loving and happy planet.

O God, help me to show through my life that this is the Planet of God. Please.

The New Genesis

And God saw that all nations of the earth, black and white, poor and rich, from North and South, from East and West, and of all creeds were sending their emissaries to a tall glass house on the shores of the River of the Rising Sun, on the island of Manhattan, to study together, to think together and to care together for the world and all its people. And God said: That is good. And it was the first day of the New Age of the earth.

And God saw that soldiers of peace were separating the combatants of quarreling nations, that differences were being resolved by negotiation and reason instead of arms, and that the leaders of nations were seeing each other, talking to each other and joining their hearts, minds, souls and strength for the benefit of all humanity. And God said: That is good. And it was the second day of the Planet of Peace.

And God saw that humans were loving the entire creation, the stars and the sun, the day and the night, the air and the oceans, the earth and the waters, the fishes and the fowl, the flowers and the herbs, and all their human brethren and sisters. And God said: That is good. And it was the third day of the Planet of Happiness.

And God saw that humans were suppressing hunger, disease, ignorance and suffering all over the globe, providing each human person with a decent, conscious and happy life, and reducing the greed, the power and the wealth of the few. And He said: That is good. And it was the fourth day of the Planet of Justice.

And God saw that humans were living in harmony with their planet and in peace with one another, wisely managing their resources, avoiding waste, curbing excesses, replacing hatred with love, greed with contentment, arrogance with humility, division with cooperation and mistrust with understanding. And He said: That is good. And it was the fifth day of the Golden Planet.

And God saw that men were destroying their arms, bombs, missiles, warships and warplanes, dismantling their bases and disbanding their armies, keeping only policemen of peace to protect the good from the bad and the normal from the mad. And God said: That is good. And it was the sixth day of the Planet of Reason.

And God saw humans restore God and the human person as the alpha and omega, reducing institutions, beliefs, politics, governments and all man-made entities to mere servants of God and the people. And he saw them adopt as their supreme law:

> You shall love the Lord your God with all your heart, all your soul, all your mind and all your strength. You shall love your neighbor as yourself. There is no greater commandment than these.

And God said: That is good. And it was the seventh day of the Planet of God.

And the Lord looked down upon the earth and said:

And now, my children, you will know again that each of you is a miracle, a unique creation in the universe, that life is a sacred gift which you must cherish at all times, that you were engendered in my image, that happiness and paradise can be established on earth, that your beautiful, miraculous planet will still spin for eons of time in the fathomless universe, that you are its caretakers and keepers, and that when finally its end comes, every atom of it will be reborn in another star in heaven. And there shall be no end to birth, life, death and resurrection in the eternal stream of the universe which you will never understand, for this will remain forever the difference between you and Me. I will now make My peace with you and let you establish a perfect Earth. Farewell, My grownup children. At long last, you are on the right path, you have brought heaven down to earth and found your proper place in the universe. I will now leave you for a long journey, for I have to turn My sight to other troubled and unfinished celestial bodies. I now pronounce you Planet of God. Be happy. Enjoy fully your divine lives on your miraculous planet with all the care, passion, ecstasy, enthusiasm and love they deserve.

* * *

As for me, before leaving this planet, I would like to say this to my human brethren and sisters:

Decide to be a spiritual person
Render others spiritual
Irradiate your spirituality
Treat every moment of your life with divine respect
Love passionately your Godgiven, miraculous life
Be endlessly astonished at your breathtaking consciousness of the universe
Thank God every moment for the tremendous gift of life
Lift your heart to the heavens always

Be a cosmic, divine being, an integral, conscious part of the universe

Contemplate with wonder the miraculous creation all around you

Fill your body, mind, heart and soul with divine trepidation

Know that you are coming from somewhere and that you are going somewhere in the universal stream of time

Be always open to the entire universe

Know yourself and the heavens and the earth

Act spiritually

Think spiritually

Love spiritually

Treat every person and living being with humaneness and divine respect

Pray, meditate, practice the art of spiritual living

And be convinced of eternal life and resurrection

About the Author

Robert Muller has been serving the United Nations for 33 years. He grew up in Alsace-Lorraine, fought in the French Resistance during World War II and was captured by the Nazis. He has performed diplomatic missions all over the world and today is Assistant Secretary-General in charge of economic and social services and the coordination of the 32 specialized agencies and world programs of the United Nations. He is also the author of *Most of All They Taught Me Happiness*.